Methuen Drama Modern Classics

The Methuen Drama Modern Plays series has always been at the forefront of modern playwriting and has reflected the most exciting developments in modern drama since 1959. To commemorate the fiftieth anniversary of Methuen Drama, the series was relaunched in 2009 as Methuen Drama Modern Classics, and continues to offer readers a choice selection of the best modern plays.

Tory Boyz

Sam, a working-class northern lad, is a Tory researcher working in the office of an education minister. Discovering that he is working in the same office in which Ted Heath originally began his career inspires Sam to research the man and the rumours about his sexuality. Through juxtaposing the two careers – Ted Heath's and that of the young, modern Tory researcher – James Graham questions whether sexuality matters in today's political world and, if it does, then why.

> 'Graham's play is about appearance and reality, about how politics is about knowing that what doesn't have to be said, doesn't have to be mended, and how, if everything is abandoned in the quest for power, then there is nothing – even love – left at all.'
>
> *Daily Telegraph*

This edition includes an introduction by Anthony Banks.

James Graham won the Catherine Johnson Award for the Best Play 2007 for *Eden's Empire*. Other plays include *Albert's Boy* (recipient of a Pearson Playwriting Bursary), *Bassett* (National Theatre Connections: Bristol Old Vic), *Little Madam* (Finborough), *Tory Boyz* (Soho Theatre), *The Man* (Finborough), *The Whisky Taster* (Bush), *Sons of York* (Finborough), *suddenlossofdignity.com* (Bush), *This House* (National Theatre), *Privacy* (Donmar Warehouse) and *The Angry Brigade* (Paines Plough). James Gra

James Graham

Tory Boyz

Introduction by Anthony Banks

Bloomsbury Methuen Drama
An imprint of Bloomsbury Publishing Plc

B L O O M S B U R Y
LONDON • NEW DELHI • NEW YORK • SYDNEY

Bloomsbury Methuen Drama

An imprint of Bloomsbury Publishing Plc

Imprint previously known as Methuen Drama

50 Bedford Square	1385 Broadway
London	New York
WC1B 3DP	NY 10018
UK	USA

www.bloomsbury.com

**BLOOMSBURY, METHUEN DRAMA and the Diana logo are
trademarks of Bloomsbury Publishing Plc**

First published 2010 by Methuen Drama as part of *Producers' Choice:
Six Plays for Young Performers*
This version first published in 2015
© 2010, 2015 James Graham

Introduction© Bloomsbury Methuen Drama 2015

British Library Cataloguing-in-Publication Data
A catalogue record for this book is available from the British Library.

ISBN: PB: 978–1–4725–8781–7
ePDF: 978–1–4725–8786–2
ePub: 978–1–4725–8782–4

Library in Congress Cataloging-in-Publication Data
A catalog record for this book is available from the Library of Congress

Series: Modern Classics

Typeset by RefineCatch Limited, Bungay, Suffolk

Introduction

Anthony Banks

James Graham is at the forefront of a generation of playwrights born in the 1980s who have a keen and persistent interest in British political history. The subjects which interest him, and the warm generous humour he employs when writing about them, could be viewed as the unlikely synthesis of the popular formulae of two of Britain's most successful political playwrights, David Hare and Alan Bennett. James Graham winningly combines the forensic scalpel of scrutiny with which Hare investigates contemporary politics and the quirky curiosity of Bennett, the Northern historian who often holds his lens up at unexpected angles on national figures. Hare and Bennett have both placed real-life state leaders from British history on stage with razor-sharp satire and warm, provocative humour: Hare's Prime Ministers range from the failing Labour leader George Jones in his play *The Absence of War* (based on Neil Kinnock) to Blair-like Alec Beasley in his play *Gethsemane* (who incidentally turns up again in his television drama *Page Eight*), to the more literal representation of Tony Blair in *Stuff Happens*; Bennett has written about a different type of state leader – monarchs: he explores *The Madness of King George III* and HMQ Elizabeth II in his play *A Question Of Attribution*. All of these plays by Hare and Bennett began their lives at the National Theatre of Great Britain in the 1980s and 1990s.

James Graham was born in Mansfield, Nottinghamshire in 1982, attended Ashfield Comprehensive School and went to Hull University in 2000 to study Drama. He wrote his first play, while still a student, for the Edinburgh Festival Fringe in 2002. *Coal Not Dole* was about the miners' strikes in the mid–1980s and it received good reviews and toured around coalfields in the spring of 2003. His next play, *Albert's Boy* in 2005, was about Einstein – the first time Graham used a 'real-life' character in one of his dramas – and was the start of a fruitful relationship with the producing theatre the Finborough in West London.

James was writer-in-residence at the Finborough from 2005 to 2009 where he wrote several plays which looked at British political history in the mid- to late-twentieth century, two of which placed British Conservative Prime Ministers on stage: *Eden's Empire* written in 2006 tells the story of Anthony Eden who was Prime Minister 1955–7, and *Little Madam* which is about Margaret Thatcher who was Prime Minister 1979–90. *Eden's Empire* uses the past to investigate the present by comparing the Suez Crisis of 1956 with the war in Iraq fifty years later. *Little Madam* uses the past to illuminate the future in a different way: it imagines Thatcher when she was twelve years old communicating with her soft toys in her bedroom who take on the personalities of colleagues we recognise later in her political career. In his review for the *Guardian*, Michael Billington explained:

> Graham rightly argues that Thatcher's psychological make-up and political instincts were the product of her childhood. The setting is the bedroom of the 12-year-old Margaret Roberts above her father's Grantham shop. Punished for rejecting her supper, the obdurate Margaret communes with her toys, who pop out of wardrobes and cupboards to prefigure her later life. So we see how the strong-willed child turns into the hard-working undergraduate, the ambitious MP and eventually the prime ministerial scourge of Keynesian interventionists, the Argentinians and the long-suffering miners.
>
> *Guardian*, October 2007

Incidentally, two more plays about Conservative Prime Ministers soon followed in London theatres: Howard Brenton featured Anthony Eden in his play about Harold Macmillan *Never So Good* at the National Theatre in 2008 and Moira Buffini presented a young and old Margaret Thatcher in conflab with the Queen in *Handbagged* at the Tricycle Theatre in 2010.

Tory Boyz is set in Westminster, in the Secretary of State's researchers' office where a few young gay Tories grapple with the tensions they find in the party's fluctuating views on openly gay ministers, especially those seeking the highest ranks, and one of them, Sam, becomes aware of the ghost of the late Prime Minister

Edward Heath, rumoured to have been a closeted homosexual, who once occupied the same office.

One of the central themes in *Tory Boyz* is state provision of education over the last decade and, in particular, the contrasts between Labour and Conservative policies. In 2000, three years into the New Labour government, the Teacher Training Agency hired advertising company McCann-Erikson to create a campaign to encourage more graduates to consider teaching as a career. The campaign ran for three years, its slogan was 'Those who can, teach' and the Teacher Training Agency claim it resulted in a fifty per cent increase in people applying for teaching courses. In the play, Nicholas spoofs this slogan in his line, 'If you're a cock, teach'. In June 2011, Education Secretary Michael Gove began education reforms which were eventually announced in full the month before the revised version of *Tory Boyz* opened in the West End. One of the key concepts of Gove's revisions to GCSE courses was a return to final examinations, rather than continuous assessment, and this became a much debated issue for ministers and educational professionals, and is referenced in this new version of *Tory Boyz*. In 2011, one year into the Conservative–Liberal coalition government, Michael Gove said:

> I think the modular system was a mistake, and the culture of re-sits is wrong. Other countries have more rigorous exams and curricula more relevant to the twenty-first century. If you are looking at the way grades are awarded, the real question is whether our exams are keeping pace with other countries. Our children will be competing for jobs with children from across the world.
>
> Michael Gove, Education Secretary,
> June 2011, reflecting on GCSE teaching in state schools

A subsidiary theme which gets a mention in Scene One of the revised version of *Tory Boyz* is the idea of Free Schools, an initiative largely supported by Michael Gove and the Conservative Party over the last five years because they believe that free schools will increase local competition and therefore raise standards of education.

As well as Education policy, the play also references young people and the extent of their interest in politics. In one of the classroom scenes, Sam tells the class, 'When you reach voting age, more of you will choose to vote in the X Factor than at the next general election'. Over the ten series of the popular television programme 'The X Factor' which ran from 2004–13, an average of ten million people tuned in each week. During the general election of 2010 there were a record number of first-time voters who took to the polls, and this was reported by many journalists to be the result of it being the first general election in which social media had played a part. However, the overall low count of first-time voters has been reported extensively in the last two general elections. According to the BBC in the 2005 general election, 37 per cent of people aged 18 to 24 voted, compared with 61 per cent of all ages.

Contextually, the most significant difference between the first version of *Tory Boyz* in 2008 and the second version in 2013 is that a general election took place in 2010 in which the Labour Party lost power and a Conservative–Liberal coalition government was put in place. This triggered James Graham to write his most popular play to date, *This House*, which again used the past to comment on the present: *This House* is about the hung parliament of 1974 and is set in the whips offices, revisiting the Palace of Westminster, a recurring setting for James Graham's plays. The play begins during Heath's administration and ends with the election of Margaret Thatcher. *This House* opened in the National Theatre's smallest auditorium, the Cottesloe, in September 2012 and the following spring transferred to the largest auditorium, the Olivier, where it was also broadcast to cinemas around the UK and the world as part of an initiative called *NT Live*. During the previous year, 2011, which saw the tenth anniversary of 9/11, James Graham wrote a play for the National Theatre's Connections youth theatre series called *Bassett* which was set in the village of Wootton Bassett in Wiltshire and examined young peoples' attitudes towards their nation being at war and the notion of national identity. A different kind of political play, it examined the consequences of Westminster on the home front in a similar way that his play *Sons Of York* had in 2007.

Another contextual difference between the first and second versions of *Tory Boyz* was the introduction of The Marriage Act (Same Sex Couples) in 2013. The bill which became known as the 'Gay Marriage Bill' received three readings and two votes in the

House of Commons. More Conservative MPs voted against gay marriage both times even though the bill received a majority 'yes' vote each time.

In *Tory Boyz*, although the main comedic drive of the play seeks to probe the confusing system of personal values of Conservative MPs and their employees with incisive wit, the play also enjoys moments when it peppers these serious themes with a lighter, flippant humour which comes out in the jocular dialogue that references the news trivia of everyday life. In an early scene, Nicholas tries to remember which celebrity chef runs the restaurant near his Berkshire parents' home where he ate at the weekend. 'Thingy McShit. Cries over chickens, curly hair.' In June 2008, just before the play opened, the *Daily Telegraph* reported: 'The chef exposed the life of an indoor broiler chicken on his Channel 4 programme, Hugh's Chicken Run. The programme, which showed Mr Fearnley-Whittingstall breaking down in tears at the sight of battery-reared chickens helped send sales of free-range chickens soaring by 40 per cent.' Two years after *Tory Boyz*, James Graham wrote another play for the National Youth Theatre about celebrity chefs called *Relish*.

Early in the play, a typical Tory is described by Nicholas as 'True blue. Home Counties, private school, cricket and rugger, huzzah.' The word 'Tory' entered British politics in 1678 – the Tories then were a royalist splinter group supporting Charles II against the Exclusion Bill proposed by the Whigs. Originally an insult, the word is derived from the medieval Irish word *tóraidh*, which means 'robber'. The modern Conservative Party was founded in 1864 by Sir Robert Peel. The Conservatives, or Tories as they are colloquially known, have increasingly attracted a reputation for being posh. In a recent party conference, held just before the West End revival of *Tory Boyz*, a panel of party members responded to the question, 'Can posh Tories ever win the working-class vote?' and the *Spectator* newspaper while covering the conference (March 2013) commented: 'Class isn't necessarily a handicap. The issue is whether voters believe that a party, or its leadership, shares their values.' Between the two first productions of *Tory Boyz*, during the general election of 2010, another play about young Conservatives was produced at the Royal Court Theatre and then in the West End, and is soon to be released as a feature film called *The Riot Club*.

The play is called *Posh*, written by Laura Wade and set in a private-dining club. The club is based on the Bullingdon Club that included David Cameron, George Osborne and Boris Johnson among its members when they were young Conservative students.

In 1991, a free weekly magazine was launched in London, targeted at the rapidly expanding social scene of gay men. Distributed nationally through bars, pubs and clubs it features adverts, gossip and news stories about celebrities, and its name is *Boyz*.

An examination of the play's title brings us to the central question and key theme in *Tory Boyz*: does being gay hamper the career of a Conservative MP? Nicholas vividly explains to Sam: '. . . there's a world of difference between the Westminster village cosmopolitan London set who get voted in and the CofE, blue rinse Daily Mail readers who *vote* them in. . . they will have a black, Islamic wheelchair bound Frenchman as Prime Minister before we ever see a fella kissing his other half on the steps of number 10.' Sam observes how Heath was forced to always 'keep his cards close to his chest.' Even in their imagined conversation over the phone at the end of the play, Sam and Heath find it almost impossible to communicate openly with each other.

Main Characters In *Tory Boyz*

Sam

I interviewed actor Simon Lennon who played Sam in the West End version of the play in 2013, this is what Simon had to say:

In rehearsals we explored why Sam was doing the job. We decided that it was because he trusted the core beliefs of the Conservative Party, and he was invested in their vision of change in the North-West of England where he comes from, that new businesses had to replace the old industries that Merseyside had been well known for, simply because we live in a changing world.

Sam is a natural leader and can take control of a group, which is clear from the way that he pragmatically handles the

school kids, but he's very uncertain within himself at the start
of the play. By the end of his journey, the audience always
found it very satisfying that he found the inner strength he
needed to stand up for what he believed was right and to
defeat the manipulative Nicholas. The scene when Nicholas
attacks Sam for 'sleeping with Labour' after he has spied
on him from the adjoining office is very telling as it shows
that Nicholas is very stuck-in-his-ways – an old school Tory,
who does not have the flexibility to be forward-thinking
and reasonable like Sam. Sam isn't all good and virtuous:
he should be a terrific role model for young gay pupil Ray,
but instead, when asked directly about his sexuality by
Ray, he bottles it, he's hopeless, he isn't able to be truthful
about his sexual orientation. In an extraordinary reversal, it
is actually Sam who needs Ray in that scene; it is Ray who
eventually leads Sam to have the courage to be honest about
who he is. This scene shows the consequences of the burden
of prejudice that Sam feels from other members of the
Conservative Party and their voters.

There is dramatic tension throughout the play and Sam is
the centre of it. It isn't until the final scene in the play when
Sam manages to get through to Ted Heath on the telephone
that he decides that he is going to be an out-and-proud gay
Conservative MP, perhaps with an eye on Number Ten.
He agrees to go out for a drink with James, the Labour
researcher who has been chasing his affections. Sam was
very satisfying to play because of that continuing dramatic
tension that he finds himself at the centre of. The power-
play between him and the other key characters is constantly
shifting. He is at the centre of the world, and the audience
rotate seeing scenes between Sam & Heath; Sam & Nicholas;
Sam & James; Sam & The schoolchildren. Although Sam
is seen to be struggling in all of these scenes, in all of these
conversations, because of the way the character has been
positioned and painted, you feel as though the audience
is on his side all the way through – that the audience's
main empathy is with Sam. I think the play achieves great
clarification in the way that it paints an uncertain, principled,

hesitant young Tory like Sam. The play is very clear about the ways that Sam is confused, why he is constantly asking questions, and why he is intrigued with the story of Heath and why he seeks communication with him. Hopefully the audience leave the theatre not with a changed view, but with clarification about the different types of Tory that exist within the party.

Nicholas

Actor Daniel Ings played Nicholas in the original production of *Tory Boyz* in 2008. This is what he had to say after watching the new version in 2013:

> *Tory Boyz* meant a lot to me in 2008 – it was the first time I really started thinking about politics. Shamefully, even at 21, I didn't really know the differences between the main political parties and the play really succeeds in giving an overview of these differences.
>
> The audiences loved hating Nicholas. We know people like him exist and wish they didn't, however while he's a character on a stage we have enough distance to laugh at the laconic charm and arrogance that has got him where he is. At the time we rehearsed the play, Boris Johnson and David Cameron were all over the news cycling to work – they were going to be the 'greenest government ever' – so we decided Nicholas should be a bike rider. When Nina drops the C-bomb at the end and Nicholas gets his come-uppance, we decided that his final moment would be putting on his bike helmet before his exit, and it remains one of the most satisfying audience reactions I've ever experienced as an actor.
>
> Politics isn't something that's taught much in schools, and political history isn't a common theme in plays written for young actors. James Graham understands and enjoys pulling apart themes and details of our political system and presenting them with clarity and in a way that's really

engaging to audiences. I think *Tory Boyz* is just as important a play as *This House* and the same can be said of both plays: they're not about good and bad or black and white – they're about ideas and human beings struggling with ideals and the contradictions within them.

The National Youth Theatre first produced *Tory Boyz* in 2008 in the run-up to the general election of 2010, and as it turns out, before the financial crisis kicked-in. The Labour government had been in power for eleven years, the economy was strong, and there wasn't the hunger for political knowledge among young people that I think has developed since.

In a way the play feels even more relevant today than it was then. There has just been a cabinet re-shuffle in which the government promoted several women, and there have been claims that this is simply an election ploy. It is still incredibly difficult for women in politics and almost impossible for openly gay people. In 2014 it seems extraordinary that this should be the case and, for that reason, *Tory Boyz* is a play that should be read, watched and talked about by not only young people, but people of all ages.

Edward Heath

Encouraged by his parents, Edward Heath started learning to play the piano in his village, Broadstairs, when he was seven; became a soloist chorister when he was nine in the local parish church; started conducting choirs at the age of fifteen; and went to Balliol College, Oxford University, as a musical scholar. At the end of his time at Oxford, war broke out and he did not feel he could take on a career in music, although he kept up his musical activities throughout his political career. 'I believe politicians shouldn't spend every minute of their lives on politics' he said in an interview in 1994. While he was Prime Minister he conducted the London Symphony Orchestra at the Royal Festival Hall in London. *Tory Boyz* opens with a prologue in which Edward Heath is seen 'conducting everything that is seen on the stage' accompanied by classical music: he literally brings the play to life. In an interview during his retirement he was asked, 'Your love for music, it's so strong, is that your true love, is that a substitute for a partner?' To which he replied 'Of course not'.

Heath's biographer John Campbell speculates that his speech, unlike that of his father and younger brother who both spoke with Kent accents, must have undergone 'drastic alteration on encountering Oxford', although retaining elements of Kent speech. The actor Niall McNamee who played Heath in the West End production explained:

> Edward Heath was probably the first Conservative Prime Minister from a working-class background. His father was a labourer. While I was researching him I found something very telling in his accent: we think of him as well-spoken 'RP'. However, if you listen closely to recordings, you can hear the Kent cockney coming through, especially in words like 'now' and 'proud'.

Reviewing in the *Daily Telegraph*, the critic Tim Walker said of McNamee: 'The actor gets Heath's shark-like smile spot on. It is a masterful performance.' McNamee wrote in his rehearsal diary:

> Heath seems to have lived a quiet, frustrated, even sad life. I think his chief frustration did not lie in his sexuality but in his struggles with being the Prime Minister. For many years after his time as PM, he was known as the incredible sulk. He believed Thatcher stabbed him in the back and she blamed him for the financial downturn. His awkward persona didn't serve him well in a time where television started to play a bigger part in political life. He seemed to make many crucial mistakes handling the troubles in Northern Ireland which cost the Tories many votes. He was pro-Europe, and frustrated that no one thanked him for joining the European Union.

Heath spent his life as a batchelor. In a BBC2 interview in 1998, he explained that he contemplated marrying childhood friend Kay Raven in the early 1950s, but that she gave up waiting for him and married an RAF officer instead. He kept her photograph in his home until his death. It can be no accident that the scene in *Tory Boyz* in which Kay tells Heath about her marriage and he realises the chances of their relationship are over takes place on Hampstead Heath, a location well-known for casual gay encounters.

Robbie

A young man on work experience in Nicholas's office, Robbie is the son of someone already working for the Conservative Party, which shows how political perspectives can be inherited. However, he is also a young southern Tory heading north to Hull University, which happens to be the university that James Graham studied at.

Structure

Most of the play takes place in the Palace of Westminster either now or during the Heath administration. The first scene, which is set in the primary location of the play – Nicholas's office – accounts for 25 per cent of the play's stage time. In this first quarter of the play, all of the play's main themes are presented. The scenes which present the early years of Edward Heath are short episodes interspersed throughout the first half of the play and are triggered by Sam's curiosity about the private life of Edward Heath. They move chronologically through his childhood and adolescence to when he is a young man in London. Each time we meet Heath, he is a little older and a little more aware of the world around him. The scenes set in the school are less frequent, but when they arrive, they are boisterous, packed with young unruly characters, and tonally contrast with the office politics of Westminster and the slight nostalgia of the scenes which trace Heath's story.

Music

Music, whether performing it, conducting it, or listening to it, is seen as something to aspire to in this play. The contrasts of melodic classical music and improvised contemporary music signify both the different sets of characters in the play, and the different levels of maturity represented, in both the past and present, and in different stages of learning and experience. In the overture to the play, the character of Heath is seen to be literally conducting the stage (some of the audience may know that Heath was a keen conductor) and they may associate the image of him conducting the stage actors and furniture as representing the formal and finely tuned way that a Prime Minister has to run a Cabinet, a government and the country. This classical music is contrasted with the unrefined brash live music which is played in the music-classroom, most notably by one of the pupils who insists on playing the drum-kit while Sam is trying to speak.

Production History

In the first decade of the twenty-first century there was a seismic increase in new plays which contained young characters at the heart of the story. The National Theatre's Connections programme, which commissions leading playwrights to create one-act plays for young people to perform, had begun in the mid-1990s and ten years on was fully established and flourishing, producing ten new scripts for young actors to perform every year at youth theatre festivals across the country. At the National Theatre itself, following the success of Alan Bennett's *The History Boys* in 2004, a comedy with a school setting, which tells the stories of eight sparky schoolboys trying to get into Oxbridge, the director of the National Theatre at the time, Nicholas Hytner, programmed six of the National Theatre's Connections plays in the Cottesloe Theatre. These had extended runs and national tours with professional young actors in 2006 and 2007, while the Royal Exchange Theatre in Manchester and the Lyric Theatre Hammersmith programmed Simon Stephens' play *Punk Rock*, which also has a school setting. There were many other plays written and produced in the mid-2000s which feature young characters in school uniforms and they were becoming very popular with audiences. The same happened on television, with serialised dramas like *Skins, Waterloo Road* and *Glee* entertaining millions of viewers of all ages. It became common for younger characters to lead dramatic storylines, on stage, and on television; the teenage characters were no longer subsidiary – they were accepted as leading figures in dramatic storylines.

The National Youth Theatre (NYT), founded in 1956, was celebrating its half century, and rather than borrowing plays from 'the adult canon' as it had done for most seasons in its first fifty years, it had begun to commission plays specifically for the 18–24 age range of their actors. The NYT began producing seasons of new plays at Soho Theatre in London, an organisation with a track record in producing fresh and provocative new writing for the stage. In 2007, the NYT enjoyed considerable success at the Soho Theatre with a season of new writing including Tanika Gupta's play *White Boy*. The following year, Paul Roseby, artistic director of the NYT, commissioned James Graham to write *Tory Boyz* for the NYT in 2008, suggesting Heath as subject matter following his successful plays at the Finborough about Thatcher, Eden and Einstein. The play received its world premiere at Soho Theatre in a production directed by Guy Hargreaves. It was revived in the version published here at the Ambassador's Theatre in London's West End in a production directed by Thomas Hescott.

Critical Response

When the play opened at Soho Theatre in August 2008, the *Guardian*'s leading theatre critic, Michael Billington, championed the new play, but doubted its central question about present-day Tory boys:

Was Edward Heath gay? If so, does it matter? According to this intriguing, contentious new play by James Graham, Heath suppressed his natural sexual instincts in order to ascend the Tory ladder. The tragedy, in Graham's reading, is that any potential gay successor would have to do much the same 50 years on. Having already written plays about Anthony Eden's ego and Margaret Thatcher's early father fixation, Graham is well equipped to turn his attention to Tory sexuality, but I jib at the play's assumption that little has really changed in 50 years. Ultimately, Graham suggests there are extra-parliamentary means of achieving one's ideals. True enough. But I still believe that the UK is now ready to accept an openly gay prime minister. Am I wrong?

Reviewing the revival for the *Guardian* in September 2013, Lyn Gardner wrote: 'Neatly entwining past and present, the play's most moving strand shows us that for a young, gay Tory the uncertainties and confusions of the past are still surprisingly current.'

All reviews were favourable when the play opened in 2008: the *Evening Standard* raved, 'Graham goes at it with fizz, flair and no small degree of humour.' *Time Out* said, 'Times are certainly changing, only a short while ago it would have been impossible to imagine the National Youth Theatre staging a play with a sympathetic gay Tory at its core.' In *Total Politics*, Conservative MP Alan Duncan wrote, '*Tory Boyz* is a one-act play of subtlety, brilliance even, whose social observation and sense of political history transfixes the audience from start to finish.'

Announcing the revised version of the play in 2013, the promotional copy written for the press release affirmed the relevance of the play's central premise:

> In the wake of the deep Conservative divide exposed by the recent vote on gay marriage, the National Youth Theatre brings its hit production back to the West End after a sold-out run at Soho Theatre in 2008. *Tory Boyz* is a bold and astute political comedy that takes us behind the scenes of the corridors of power at Westminster where saving face and avoiding scandal is the order of the day.

Reviewing the 2013 revival, critic Libby Purves said, 'It was a smart move to revive (with the author's skilful updates) James Graham's 2008 play about the Conservative Party and gay rights' and Tim Walker, reviewing for the *Daily Telegraph* wrote:

> As David Cameron can no doubt ruefully attest, Europe and homosexuality continue to discomfit his party. No wonder Sir Edward Heath, the bachelor who took the nation into Europe, is the prime minister whose name few Conservatives dare to speak these days. James Graham's updated *Tory Boyz* posits

the case that the Conservative machine is more or less run by homosexuals. Graham's play is about appearance and reality, about how politics is about knowing that what doesn't have to be said, doesn't have to be mended, and how, if everything is abandoned in the quest for power, then there is nothing – even love – left at all.

A Timeline of Dates and Events

1916   Edward Heath born in Broadstairs, Kent.
1935–39   Edward Heath studies Politics, Philosophy & Economics at
            Balliol College, Oxford University.
1956   National Youth Theatre founded by Michael Croft.
1968   Theatres Act abolishes stage censorship.
1970–74   Edward Heath Prime Minister of Great Britain.
1982   James Graham born in Mansfield, Nottinghamshire.
1998   Edward Heath is one of only seventeen Conservative MPs
            who vote 'yes' to lowering the age of consent for gay sex to the
            age of 16.
2000–03   James Graham studies Drama at the University of Hull.
2004   Civil Partnerships become legal in the UK.
2005   10th June: Openly gay MP Alan Duncan stands for the
            leadership of the Conservative Party, he soon withdraws due to
            lack of internal support.
            17th July: Edward Heath dies.
            10th August: *Albert's Boy* by James Graham opens at the
            Finborough Theatre London.
2006   Liberal Democrat MPs Mark Oaten and Simon Hughes
            announce they will stand in the leadership contest to replace
            Charles Kennedy. Oaten withdraws and resigns ten days
            later when the *News Of The World* reveals he had hired male
            prostitutes. Four days later, *The Sun* reveals that Simon Hughes
            has been calling a gay chatline.
            Eden's Empire by James Graham opens at the Finborough Theatre
            London and wins the Catherine Johnson award for Best Play.
2007   *Little Madam* by James Graham opens at the Finborough
            Theatre London.
2008   *Tory Boyz* opens at Soho Theatre London, directed by Guy
            Hargreaves.
            Sons Of York by James Graham opens at the Finborough
            Theatre London.
2010   *Posh* by Laura Wade opens at The Royal Court Theatre
            London.
            Relish by James Graham opens at the Tramshed, London,
            directed by Paul Roseby.

2011	*Bassett* by James Graham a play about a nation at war, set in Wootton Bassett, Wiltshire, is performed as part of the National Theatre's Connections youth theatre series around the country and also at Bristol Old Vic to mark the tenth anniversary of 9/11.
2012	*This House* by James Graham opens in the Cottesloe, National Theatre London.
2013	July: The Queen grants royal assent to The Marriage Act (Same Sex Couples) 2013.
	September: *Tory Boyz* opens in revised version at the Ambassadors Theatre in London's West End, in a season alongside *Romeo & Juliet* and Michael Lesslie's new play *Prince Of Denmark*.
2014	*Privacy* by James Graham opens at the Donmar Warehouse. *Finding Neverland* by James Graham opens at ART Boston USA.
	The Angry Brigade by James Graham opens at Theatre Royal Plymouth.
2015	The broadcast of James's Channel 4 drama about Nick Clegg, depicting the formation of the coalition government in 2010.

Tory Boyz was first performed by the National Youth Theatre
Company at the Soho Theatre, London, on 21 July 2008. The cast
was as follows:

Sam	Shaun Rivers
Nicholas	Dan Ings
Nina	Sair Khan
Robbie	James Camp
James	Sam Marks
Douglas	Chris Greenwood
Ted Heath	Hamish McDougall
Mrs Heath	Clare Harlow
Miss Locke	Beatrice Walker
Timothy	Robert Willoughby
Frank	Dan Walton
Kay	Alice Bailey Johnson
Tommo	Sope Dirisu
Shayne	Tom Aslett
Muznah	Taura Marston
Heather	Mia Hatfield
Michelle	Clara Nortey
Ray	Daniel Ward
Adam	Louis Lasa Tarbuck
Young Teddy	James Musgrave
Young John	Robert Willoughby
Young Kay	Mia Hatfield
Kids	James Camp, Sair Khan
	Dan Walton,
	Chris Greenwood

Director   Guy Hargreaves
Lighting Designer   David Kidd
Video Designer   John Lloyd-Fillingham
Sound Designer   Jonathan Jones

A new version was first performed by National Youth Theatre at the Ambassadors Theatre, London, on 23 September 2013. The cast was as follows:

Sam	Simon Lennon
Nicholas	Sope Dirisu
Nina	Anna Spearpoint
Robbie/Adam/Timothy	James Laurence Hunter
James/Shayne	Tom Prior
Douglas/Frank	Tom Thompson
Ted Heath	Niall McNamee
Mrs Heath/Teaching Assistant	Aruhan Galieva
Miss Locke	Daisy Whalley
Kay	Louisa Beadel
Tommo/Young John	Miguel Brooking
Muznah	Zainab Hasan
Heather	Abigail Rose
Michelle	Sophie Ellerby
Ray	Aaron Gordon
Director	Thomas Hescott
Designer	James Button
Lighting Designer	Ian Fincher
Sound Designer	Mick Livermore

Tory Boyz

Characters

Sam	Parliamentary Researcher, Male, 23, North West.
Nicholas	Chief of Staff, Late 20s, South East.
Nina	PA, 22, London.
Robbie	Intern, 19, London.
James	Labour Parliamentary Researcher, 20s.
Douglas	Librarian

Tommo	Male, 15/16, GCSE student.
Shayne	Male, 15/16, GCSE student.
Muznah	Female, 15/16, GCSE student.
Heather	Female, 15/16, GCSE student.
Michelle	Female, 15/16, GCSE student.
Ray	Male, 15/16, GCSE student.
Adam	Male, 15/16, GCSE student.
Teaching Assistant	

Ted Heath	Joint Deputy Whip, Male.
Mrs Heath	Ted's Mum, 20s/30s.
Miss Locke	Ted's piano teacher, 17.
Timothy	Junior Whip, Male, 20s.
Frank	Junior Whip, Male, 20s.
Kay	Ted's friend, Female.

Young Teddy / Teenage Teddy
Young John
Young Kay
Kids

Many of the roles can be doubled – for example, the modern day GCSE students can become the younger children of the 1950s (as indicated in the text), Librarians can be Junior Whips and so on, or alternatively just cast one actor per individual part.

Notes on the Text

A slash mark / indicates the character with the next line should begin speaking, overlapping with the preceding character.

(text within a bracket) indicates that the line is spoken softly or internal.

This edition contains the 2013 updated text of the play, which differs from that published as part of *Producers' Choice: Six Plays for Young Performers* in 2010.

Spotlight on a music stand, holding song sheets.

Ted Heath *enters to applause. He bows to the audience. The applause dies. He turns to face the dark stage.*

As he flicks his baton, individual parts of the scene light up, accompanied by a musical instrument – for example, one flick lights a desk lamp, accompanied by a flute, before darkness again. Another lights a phone, which sounds a ring. Another, a spot on the filing cabinet accompanied by a tuba etc. – as though the 'scene' were an orchestra warming up.

Objects and areas begin to light up of their own accord, interrupting each other. **Ted** *taps the stand for silence, regaining control.*

He lifts his arms grandly . . . and begins. Characters enter and are 'conducted' by **Ted**. *Parliamentary researchers answer phones, open filing cabinets; school children fight, dance, play . . . the music reaches a climax,* **Ted** *drops his arms, the music cuts out, and he disappears.*

Sam's Office, The Houses of Parliament.

Two desks. Computers, phones, papers scattered around. A few chairs. A closed door to an adjoining office. A flip chart with a handwritten list of 'TEACHERS UNIONS' including NUT, NASUWT, NAHT, GTC, ASCL and ATL. **Sam** *is at his desk, on the phone, in mid flow . . .*

Sam   . . . so in principle, yes, just concerns over implementation.

And resources, of course.

Nicholas, *Chief of Staff, enters slovenly, sighing, holding a packet of crisps, a bottle of water and a tabloid newspaper, which he tosses onto a nearby desk.*

Nicholas (*yawning*)   Well that was a bag of wank. (*Sees* **Sam** *on the phone*). Sorry.

Sam   And what about our proposal to favour final exams as the primary means of assessment?

Great. Well. Thanks for your time. That's been really useful. Thanks. Bye.

Nicholas (*stretching, referencing the flip chart*)   Ticking them off, Sammy boy?

Sam (*puts the phone down and goes to the board*)   Yep. The pupil premium is proving pretty – Jesus, tongue twister or what?

Nicholas (*laughs*)   'The Pupil Premium / is Proving –'

Sam   Pupil premium is proving pretty popular across the board.

Nicholas (*sighs, looks at it*)   And what a board, Christ. Gives me shivers just looking at it. Hated school.

Sam   You picked the wrong guy to research for, then.

Nicholas   MPs are like venereal diseases, Sam, you don't pick them, they pick you.

Sam   Is that medically true?

Nicholas   Are *you* medically true?

Sam   Next reshuffle, he's staying put, this is his passion.

Nicholas (*at this computer, starting it up*)   Bollocks, that's just gas and air – is that what I mean?

Sam   Piss and wind?

Nicholas   Piss and wind. What's gas and air?

Sam   What they give to women in labour. The 'giving birth', not the 'political party'.

Nicholas   Fucking should give women in Labour gas and air.

Sam (*mock gasps*)   That's not PC.

Nicholas   I know, it's an Apple Mac. / Whey!

Sam (*recognising his pun*)   Whey!

Nicholas   Thank you Westminster! I'm here all week.
Un-fucking-fortunately.

Come on then, brief me so I can bullshit my way through this.
The hell is NASUWT again? National –

Sam   National Association of Schoolteacher's Union of Women
Teachers –

Nicholas   Lah la-lah la-lah. NUT, GLT, ABC, one two three.
Jesus Christ, I'm bollocksed, man. Never a good night's sleep,
Sundays, is it. And I've just had (*dramatically*) 'the morning from
hell'. So. (*Slumps into a chair. Swivels*).

'N-U-T'. Urgh. Laugh a minute, it was not. If you can, do, if
you're a cock, teach.

Sam   Anything to bring up in committee?

Nicholas   Nah, sod 'em, they're just here for day out, happy to
get a tour of the palace. 'Gosh isn't it old and pretty and will I get
to go up Big Ben –'

Sam   Did you explain that Big Ben was the bell.

Nicholas   I explained that you were the bell.

Sam   Good one.

Nicholas (*checking his phone*)   What date is it. Man, where is this
year going? Oop! Look, look at this, little notification on the old
calendar here, Sam.

Sam   What?

Nicholas   You know what. Village drinks tonight. You going?

Sam   Offered to do a stint at the press office.

Nicholas (*laughs, shaking his head*)   Course you did.

Sam   What does that mean?

Nicholas   Means you make me laugh, Sam. And what about the
big shindig, reception thing, that's this afternoon isn't it?

Sam   So?

Nicholas   So. You going?

Sam   I've got my workshop at the school today, and anyway why would I be going?

Nicholas   Coz. Big deal, innit. Historic. (*Arm in the air*). Be loud and proud.

Sam   What do you . . .? Why . . .? It's not some club, Nick. You don't just get invited along because you're –

Nicholas   All right, Tetchy Von Sensitive. (*As 'street'*). Relax, fam, you get me. (*Referencing the adjoining office*). Is he in?

Sam   No he's still in committee.

Nicholas   Oh, Shizer Chiefs. Well he'll be a delight this afternoon then. (*Opens his crisps, with his newspaper*). Urgh. Questions, questions, since when was the front page about asking questions instead of just reporting the news?

'Are there more Poles in Britain that British?' No.

Phone rings. **Sam** *answers.*

Sam   Hello?

Nicholas   'Is there a paedophile in you son's bedroom right now' No, it's all fine, actually, / thanks. Just carry on.

Sam   Four o' clock. OK. Bye. (*Phone down*).

Nina *enters.* **Nicholas** *stands to greet her with mock-adoration.*

Nina   Afternoon.

Nicholas   Ah, there she is. How are we, how are we? What's that?

Nina   Baguette.

Nicholas (*imitating*)   'Baguette'. What kind? / What kind of baguette?

Nina (*handing to* **Sam**)   Here, OFSTED. Rest are online.

Sam   Ta.

Nina   Tuna Nicoise.

Nicholas   Tuna Nicoise, tres bon, tres bon. (*Taking her hand and hold it out, looking at her outfit*). Like this little number, today, Nina. 'You're bringing sexy back'.

Nina   Worn it before, dead old.

Nicholas   First time I've seen it, though.

Nicholas *spins her as he sings.* **Nina** *laughs and groans, not fully cooperating.*

Nicholas   'The first time . . . ever I saw your face.'

Nina   Do you mind?

Nicholas (*looking at her hand, gasping playfully*)   And what is this, Nina, Nina, ballerina, no ring, no ring, on your pretty little finger, oh no! Weekend in the Cotswolds not go quite to plan, this is terrible. Time you moved on, ey Sam?

Nina   Look, it's fine, yeah? Just –

Nicholas   Sam's in one of them, today.

Sam   In what?

Nicholas   In one of them moods.

Sam   I'm busy, if that's what you mean.

Nicholas   No, that isn't what I mean, but never mind. (*Sympathetic groan*). Oh Nina.

Nina   Genuinely don't want to talk about it, and I'm gonna get annoyed in a sec. So.

Nicholas   Well *I* . . . (*Wanders, opening his bottle of water*). . . . I had a fabulous weekend, children. I went to that guy's restaurant, near the 'rents house, in lovely Berkshire, and I cannot quite describe to you this menu. / It had –

Sam   Whose restaurant is it?

Nicholas   What's his face's – (*the baguette*) that absolutely stinks, Nina.

Nina   Deal with it. Whose restaurant?

Nicholas   Thingy McShit. Cries over chickens, curly hair. Blooming . . . Bloomingdale.

Nina   Blumenthal.

Nicholas   Blumenthal.

Sam   You're thinking of Whittingstall. Curly hair.

Nicholas   No, this is Bloomingdale.

Nina/Sam   Blumenthal.

Nicholas   Blumenthal! Fuck's sake! Right. Listen to this. (*Holds out his left hand*). Bacon. (*Holds out his right hand*). Ice cream. (*Puts his hands together as 'one'*).

Nina   Bollocks.

Nicholas   Na-ah. Na-ah. Bacon ice cream. (*As* Peter Kay). 'I've tasted it, it's the future.'

Sam   Sounds ridiculous.

Nicholas   Your face is ridiculous.

Nina   I don't believe you.

Nicholas   Don't care if you believe me, I'm not saying it to impress you, I'm saying it to inform you. Whether or not you learn and grow is up to you.

Robbie *enters, apologetically.*

Robbie   Nina, sorry. You've got a, um –

Nicholas   Ah-ha! And who's this? Our next intern extraordinaire, come in, come in.

Nina   Robbie, Nicholas; Nicholas, Robbie. Don't listen to a word he says.

Nicholas 'Don't listen to a . . .'. (*Tuts*). Hi Robbie. (*Shaking*). Nicholas. And you know Saint Sam-u-el over here?

Robbie. Uh, yeah, we, we briefly. Met. Uh, Nina, sorry, there's a lobby correspondent with a photographer outside, asking –

Nicholas A what? Why?

Robbie He says he's here for something else, some ceremony thing.

Nicholas Oh yeah, gay wedding, down in the chapel.

Robbie A gay . . . what, here? In Parliament? Like . . . two men?

Nicholas That's normally how gay works, Robbie.

Nina Unless it's two women.

Nicholas All right, Emily fucking . . . (*Sighs, can't think, gestures for help*).

Nina Dickinson.

Nicholas Dickinson, thank you.

Robbie Why would they want to get married in Parliament?

Nicholas Why not, the law that allowed it was passed here, ey Sammy boy? Fitting.

Nina It's two MPs, Robbie, that's why.

Robbie Oh. Right. Well he, the camera, guy, he wants to quickly nab a pic of the office if he can?

Nina Why? / No, he can . . .

Nicholas Ah! (*Mock 'ner-ner' childish*). 'I know what this is'. *Today* programme, this morning. Talking about the wedding today, and one the presenters brought up the whole Ted Heath thing again.

Robbie What Ted Heath thing?

Nicholas That he was gay.

Sam Fuck's sake.

Nina   What's that got to do with us?

Nicholas   This used to be his office.

Nina   Did it?

Nicholas   One of them, yeah. Right –

Robbie   He was gay?

Sam   Nobody knows do they, it, it's –

Robbie   We've had a gay Prime Minister and no one talks about it, that's amazing.

Nicholas   That's because we're British, Robbie, we don't mind pushing the boundaries so long as afterwards (*whispering, exaggeratedly*) we absolutely never talk about it even though everybody definitely knows, sssshh.

(*To* **Nina**, *leaving*). Come on, then.

Nina   This really used to be his office?, why didn't I know that?

Nicholas   Jesus Neen, every office used to be someone else's and these have been offices for centuries, we're probably breathing in about twenty dead Prime Ministers.

Nina *and* **Nicholas** *leave.* **Robbie** *watches them go, unsure whether or not to stay.* **Sam** *has a glance at him before continuing to shift, staple, move, sign etc.*

Robbie   So. You're not your average Tory.

Sam   Really.

Robbie   You've got an accent.

Sam   Ah. *You've* got an accent.

Robbie   You've got a northern accent.

Nicholas *has re-entered.*

Sam   / Yes. I do.

Nicholas   Shame, he's buggered off. Do what?

Sam   Yes I do have a northern accent.

Nicholas   Yeah, sorry about him, he's like a genetic deformity. And there's no cure, unfortunately. Me, though, I'm true blue. Home Counties, private school, cricket and rugger, huzzah. That more what you expected?

Robbie   Pretty much. (*Beat*). So. Ted Heath was gay, then? Shit. And Conservative as well.

Nicholas   Lesson one, Robert, the Tory party is the gayest party, by about a country mile. Certainly behind the scenes, our lot, and certainly in London. The whole machine survives on them.

Robbie   I've never met a gay Tory.

Nicholas   Sam's gay.

Robbie   Are you?

Sam (*shoots* **Nicholas** *a look; short pause*)   If it matters.

Nicholas   Oy, no one's saying it matt– . . . the boy was only asking, you prickly fucktard. He might be gay, all we know. Are you?

Robbie   Uh. (*Pause. Shrugs*). Dunno. A bit.

Nicholas   A . . .? You're . . .?

Robbie (*pause. Laughs, embarrassed*)   Uh, sorry, that – that was weird, I, I, don't –

Nicholas (*pause, unnerved he may have crossed a line*)   No, that's . . . don't – sorry –

Robbie   I've no idea what I meant, sorry, it – I . . .

Nicholas   No honestly, I shouldn't have . . . (*Pause*). No, there's a, um . . . isn't there, Sam, a, like a Westminster gay night. Tonight. 'Village Drinks', a monthly gay, er . . . very popular. Even the straight ones feel obliged. God and you should see the gay disco at the end of the party conference. Something to, uh . . . behold.

Robbie   God, I never would have imagined. Always thought that was more their thing. The other side.

Nicholas   Nah it's a myth, but don't tell Joe Public, it suits us to be the stuffy, traditional lot sometimes, makes people feel safe. Something constant in a world of change. Fact is – Sam, turn your capacity to get offended down to 1 for a second, right?

Sam   Or maybe turn your capacity to be reasonable and polite up to 10 instead?

Nicholas   Sorry mate, dial's broken – fact is, Rob, lot of that lot still have to come at it all 'pie and a pint' brigade, working class, tough, no messing, whereas most of our lot, they're like Oscar Wilde characters, all got sent off to boarding school as kids, probably didn't get to see a girl till they were like 18 and so they were shit scared of them.

Sam   I'm not going to bite –

Nicholas   And on our side the Old Boy's network still means something, so you can toss your mate off and know it won't go any further.

Sam   Oh come on!

Nicholas   Ahh! (*Imitates a winding in a fishing rod*). He took the bait. Easy does it, easy does it, wind him in.

It's true, though. And I'm allowed to say it 'cause I'm not the picture postcard Tory either.

Sam   Maybe there isn't a picture postcard anymore, maybe that's why got back into power.

Robbie   Except you didn't.

Nicholas   Sorry.

Robbie   Well you . . . you didn't win, did you. You're . . . sharing it.

Nicholas   Well seeing as you're going to be working with our 'special friends' (*at his watch*) in fact we're got at 3 o'clock at the DofE –

Sam   4 o' clock –

Nicholas   I've got down 3pm –

Sam   Changed, sent you an email –

Nicholas   Haven't checked my emails, (*not serious, eating his crisps*) I've just been run off my feet ever since I got in. Thing you need to know about the Coalition, Rob, is it's like foreplay, nothing more. You have to pretend you're interested in making them happy, a little stroke here, bit of what's-it-called, dry humping there, I want to say fromage but that's a cheese –

Sam   Maybe this isn't appropriate, Nicholas?

Nicholas   Either way, the point is, yes, we have to give the Lib Dems a little tickle but we're not obliged to make 'em cum, does that make sense?

Robbie   Erm, yes, that's really clear, thank you.

Nicholas (*standing, packing*)   Anything other questions? Getting on OK?

Robbie   Yeah, you know, fine. It's just been coffee and photocopying, but –

Nicholas   Well it doesn't get much more exciting than that, I'm afraid *The West Wing*, this ain't. You had a tour of the place?

Robbie   Yeah, a brief one. It's weird. Loads of cafés, and gyms and bars. / So many bars.

Nicholas (*laughs*)   Avoid the Sports and Social, that's where the old school Labour's guzzle down their real ale. We tend to go Bellamy's, don't we?

Sam (*busy*).

Nicholas   Well, Sam doesn't have a life but you'll likely find a lot of us lot there.

Robbie   Yeah, and that's what's . . . I can't – you're all so young.

Nicholas   Hire that man! (*Laughs*). No, it's because, in all seriousness, the pay's pretty rubbish. Just to warn you. The MPs, they nab us as graduates desperate to get on any ladder as researchers, PAs, dogsbodies, and by the time we hit our late twenties, we're bored and underpaid and so we leave or get headhunted and off we pop to earn some real money. I'll be leaving soon, God willing. But Sam here, he's been told he could have the pick of the bunch if he stays. CRD. CCHQ.

Nina (*re-enters*)   Those reports are ready for binding, Robbie, if you want.

Robbie   Uh, yeah. Cool. Sorry. Thank you. (*Exit*).

Nina *perches on her desk, eating her baguette.* **Sam** *still busying around them.*

Nicholas (*raising an eyebrow at* **Nina**).

Nina (*chuckling*)   What?

Nicholas   Nice, your boy there.

Nina   Piss off. Just nice to have someone being keen for a change.

Nicholas   Oh God, he's not one of these that 'believes' in things, is he?

Sam   I believe in things.

Nicholas   That's what I mean.

Sam *gets a text message on his phone. He reads it.*

Nicholas   (Can't be doing with two fucking Ghandis, drive me nuts.)

Sam   It's him.

Nina *and* **Nicholas** *stand into 'work' mode. A distinct sense of efficiency now.*

Nicholas   What's he need?

Sam (*reading*)   'Free school, Hertfordshire question mark, name and results asap. Can't find.'

Nicholas (*moving to computer but pointing behind him to files as he goes*)   In there?

Nina (*retrieving them*)   No, he took them up, I'm sure.

Nicholas (*typing*)   I'll get the name, then Sam you phone for results.

Sam (*with a Blackberry*)   They'll be listed on the website. /
(What was the name?)

Nicholas   Ah 'Wikipedia', what would we do without you?

Sam (*searching her files*)   I wanna say St Mary's, St M-m-m –

Nicholas (*reading the screen*)   Actually, I'll check local newspapers.

Nina (*with lists, running her finger down*)   Hertfordshire schools,
here.

Nicholas   Good.

Sam (*found it*)   Got it. St Mary's-in-the-Field. Local resident
trust school established '07.

Nicholas   Eureka. (*Begins typing*).

Nina   Got it as well. (Phone Number . . .). (*Dialling on the phone*).

Nicholas   Here we go. (*Searching screen*). Results, results. Come
on. Shit, shit, shit.

Sam (*pointing to the screen*)   There. (*Texting as he reads*).

Nicholas   Well done, well done.

Nina   We good? (*Putting the phone down*).

Nicholas   Sam?

Sam (*sending the message*)   Yep.

Nicholas (*reading*)   And doing very well. Seventy-two percent
grades A-C, blimey.

Sam   OK. Sent.

Nicholas   Weuw! (*Standing*). Well done, ladies. (*Stretching*).
Fuck, I think that's me done for the day now, Jesus.

Robbie *enters again.*

Robbie   Nina, sorry, there's / a –

Nicholas   Stop apologising, Robbie, this is the House of Commons for Christ's sake.

Robbie   Oh. OK, sorry. Nina, there's a call for you.

Nina   Thank you. (*Exits*).

Robbie (*to* **Nicholas**)   Sorry. (*Exits*).

Nicholas   'Sorry'. 'Sorry'. Jesus. Apologises more than Boris.

Sam   Thanks for that.

Nicholas   What?

Sam   Earlier.

Nicholas   What the fuck is your fucking problem today? Go get some lunch.

Sam   He's still in there, might text down again.

Nicholas   I'm on it. (*Drinking some more water. Watching him*). Oy.

Sam   What?

Nicholas   Be happier.

Sam   Be . . .? I don't know what that means. What does that mean?

Nicholas   You know what that means. Be nicer. He was only trying to be nice.

Sam   I was only trying to be nice.

Nicholas   Try harder. (*Beat. Drinks*). Sam? (*Serious*). Try harder. When you get this busy you get distracted with people. Forget minor courtesies.

Sam   Like what.

Nicholas   Like smiling. Remember what it was to smile, Sam?

Sam   I'm smiling now.

Nicholas   Smiles have teeth, Sam. See. (*Smiles*).

Sam (*smiles a grotesquely 'teethy' grin*).

Nicholas *mimics him, more grotesquely, and* **Sam** *mimics him back. They stop, and smile genuinely at each for a sec over the silliness of this, before returning.*

Nicholas   Oy.

Sam (*sighs, looking up again*).

Nicholas   He isn't a threat. He's just a boy.

Sam (*beat, stops what he's doing*)   Now I'm really sure I don't know what that means.

A moment, **Sam** *and* **Nicholas** *looking at each other,* **Nicholas** *swigging from his bottle.* **Robbie** *enters and smiles, waiting, as though to continue whatever it was they were doing before.* **Nicholas** *makes to leave.*

Nicholas   Sam, as you're clearly not going to lunch, why not give Roberto here a whirlwind tour of the life of a parliamentary researcher. I'll be upstairs.

Nicholas *leaves.* **Sam** *continues with his work for a while.*

Robbie   So he's your boss.

Sam   He's the Chief of Staff. Michael One has four –

Robbie (*pointing to the adjoining office*)   Michael One?

Sam   No. Two Michael's. Michael One, Secretary of State, our guy, Michael Two, coalition partner, is the minister underneath. I'm Michael One's Researcher, Nina his PA and Nicholas is Chief of Staff.

Robbie (*momentarily stunned by the sharpness of the answer*)   'K. And what do you do?

Sam (*beat. Realising he's not going to get out of not talking, stop what he's doing. 'Nicer'*)   You a first year undergrad?

Robbie   Will be. Just done my 'A' Levels. Dad's Honorary Chairmen of Reading West association. Thought it'd be good me getting some experience.

Sam   PPE?

Robbie   Yeah. In Hull. Wherever the fuck that is. Didn't even go to the open day.

Sam   End of the M62, east coast. After you pass (what is it?) Pontefract, it's like the only thing left at the end. So by that point all the cars on the road have to be going to Hull or else drive straight on into the North Sea. Which to be fair, when they see Hull, a lot of people actually do.

Robbie (*laughs*).

Sam (*to himself, sarcastically*)   See, happy, jokes.

Robbie   So. Do you reckon he was gay then or what? Ted Heath.

Sam   I don't think it changes anything, do you?

Robbie   Why do you think he kept it hidden. If he was, I mean.

Sam   Well I would have thought that was obvious. He wanted to be Prime Minister. But things have moved on.

Robbie   Cool. So it's never been a problem? For you, I mean. Being here.

Sam   Hasn't yet.

Robbie (*beat*)   Cool. Well. Maybe I'll see you at that drinks thing tonight then, if everyone's going.

Sam   No I'm doing a stint in the press office. Always got to be someone on late. 'Case the Queen dies or something.

Robbie   Right-oh. Oh well. (*Beat*). I'd better . . . get back to it, then.

Sam (*smiling, dryly*)   Okay dokey.

Pause. **Robbie** *leaves.* **Sam** *has gathered his things and closes up his bag.*

Ted Heath *appears, faintly, almost an apparition, on the phone at the opposite desk. His voice like an echo, hardly distinguishable.* **Sam** *watches before exiting.*

House of Commons Library.

Douglas, *an assistant librarian, is collecting some papers.* **Sam**
enters.

Douglas   Hullo.

Sam   Hi. Erm. I just have . . . (*Unfolding a note and handing it over*)
. . . couple of extra reports for Michael we need pulling, if that's OK.

Douglas   Roger, roger. Pick up tomorrow morning, all right?

Sam   Thanks. (*Making to leave. Stops. Awkward*). Douglas, you
. . . you've not been . . . you haven't heard anything about this new,
uh . . . new Ted Heath stuff? Have you?

Douglas   Oh I don't pay attention to gossip, Sam. I'm surrounded
by one of the most comprehensive banks of knowledge imaginable.
Why waste time with rumour when I can make a withdrawal of
hard facts? (*Laughs*).

Sam   OK. Cool.

Douglas   Course I will say this. My Granddad always used to
speak very highly of him.

Sam   Oh yes of course, 'cause he –

Douglas   Nearly thirty years here. Left when the Lady came to
power. Now, he did say he was a very private man, hard to know
unless he . . . you know, unless he let you in. Nice enough. But . . .
you know. One of them. Bit funny.

Sam   Right. (Right). Uh, thanks. Douglas. (*Exiting*).

Douglas   I could give you a couple of interesting exhibits, mind.
If you were . . . interested.

Sam (*stops. Turns. Considers . . .*)

A Music Classroom. Secondary School.

*Some chairs, a couple of tables. A piano, keyboard, drum kit,
other instruments dotted around. Noise approaching from outside.*

Tommo *bursts in and tosses his rucksack in anger. He's followed in by* **Ray***,* **Shayne** *and* **Muznah***, laughing.*

Tommo   Just fuck off, yeah?

Ray   Awh man, that was fucking ace!

Muznah   No lie, that is the most hilarious thing I / have ever seen. Fact!

Ray   Serious, bruv! You gotta come see, he's still down.

Tommo   I ain't going back out there, no way, no fucking way.

Shayne   Why not, he can't hit for shit, man. Clearly. / You had him.

Tommo   He'll knock me out next time, swear – oh my gosh, what have I done?

Muznah   Don't be a fool, he just knocked himself out, innit.

Ray (*laughing, clapping his hands and hopping around*)   I cannot believe, cannot believe.

Shayne (*joining him and slapping hands, pissing himself*)   Shit man . . .

Tommo   Yeah, you laugh, it's all right for you, innit.

Tommo *sits down at a drum kit and begins bashing, kicking it.* **Heather** *and* **Michelle** *enter.*

Heather   What just happened?

Muznah   / Tommo, yeah –

Michelle   Why the fuck is Trip lying / lying on the ground?

Heather   Tommo?

Ray   No, he didn't do nothing, he didn't get a chance. Trip punched *himself* in the head!

Michelle   What?

Ray   Swear to God. He squares up to Tommo, yeah –

Tommo   Ray, leave it!

Ray   Proper up in his face, giving it all sumfin about Tommo's brother and Trip's sister –

Shayne   Awh / seriously? Your Mark has been mashing his sister?

Ray   Tommo pushes him, and we're all like, 'fuck man'.

Michelle   Ohmygod, / you pushed Trip?

Ray   Tommo's gonna die, yeah? Trip pulls his arm back, like this, ready to go in, but he, obviously didn't reckon on Rocky having knocked him so hard, wobbling, right? And he goes in . . . (*Laughing, imitating*), punches *himself*, back of the head.

Michelle *and* **Heather** *burst into hysterics. Even* **Tommo** *smiles now.*

Shayne (*slaps* **Tommo** *on the chest*).   Mate, you're like, the only person in the history of the world to knock Trip to the ground.

Tommo   He knocked himself to the ground!

Muznah   Man, you gotta get back out there, take a bow. (*As a boxing call*). 'The undefeated champion of the / woooorld!'

Tommo   Fuck that, no way.

Heather (*looking out though the door*)   Oy, he's up, walking around now.

Tommo (*pacing, afraid*)   Awh shit, man. *Shit.*

Heather   Smedley's with him.

Shayne (*calling out*)   'Fattie'. / 'Fattie Smeders!'

Muznah   Ah, Trip looks well embarrassed. / He's bright red!

Ray   He fucking should be. (*Imitates punching himself again*).

Heather   Adam's here.

Ray (*running over*)   Wait. Ssh.

Michelle   Heather, how did we miss that? Gutted!

Ray *has run to hide behind the door.* **Adam** *walks in.* **Ray** *jumps him, playfully but aggressively, from behind, trying to mount him.*

Ray   Yo Adam, man!

Adam   Argh, fuck off Ray!

Ray   Oh come on, you know you like it, don't lie. You've gotta be true to yourself, innit.

Adam (*scrambling free*)   Fuck off! Serious. Takes the piss. Why does he do it, why? Gay.

Ray   You're gay.

Adam   You are.

Michelle *has hooked up her iPod to some portable speakers. A track plays. Everyone except* **Tommo** *and* **Adam** *jump up and begin to dance around.* **Michelle** *skips forward in the song and turns it up loud before joining them.* **Shayne** *sits at the drum and begins bashing.*

Sam *enters with a* **Teaching Assistant**. *One by one* **Adam**, **Heather, Michelle**, **Tommo**, **Muznah** *and finally* **Ray**, *clock him and stop.* **Michelle** *stops the music.*

Teaching Assistant   5b?

Michelle   Yeah.

Teaching Assistant (*to* **Sam**)   5b. The clip-boards over there and, uh . . . (*Handing him marker pens)* keep hold of these. I'll leave you to it. (*Exits*).

Sam   Thank you. (*Pause. Surveys the scene*). Hey.

Shayne   Hey.

Michelle   Hello.

Sam   I'm Sam. How you all doing, all right?

Michelle   All right thank you. How are you?

Ray   Are you our politician man?

Sam   I am your politician man, yes. Except I'm not a politician.

Muznah   But you work at Downing Street, innit.

Sam   No, I work in the Houses of Parliament.

Ray   Like Big Ben?

Sam   Well, the palace where Big Ben is, yes. Big Ben is actually the name of the bell but –

Shayne   Ey, you know the bottom of a bell, sir, do you call that the 'bell-end'?

Sam   I'm a researcher for the Conservative Party on schools and children. In fact I'm, I'm one of four people who knows more about Conservative educational policy than anyone else in the country. So . . .

Muznah (*sarcastic, mock-interested*)   Is it?

All (*snigger*).

Shayne   Wait, you're a Tory? Awh, man. I thought we was gonna get a Labour.

Ray   Aren't Tories all posh and old, sir?

Sam   No, I'm a Tory, do I sound posh or look old?

Tommo   No, you sound a bit like a pikey.

Michelle (*hits him*).

Sam   I'm from Liverpool.

Ray   Ain't that a right shit hole?

Sam   No more than anywhere else.

Tommo (*trying to imitate a Liverpudlian accent*)   'Hello. I'm from Liverpool. Go on Gerrard, go on Saurez. Ay, ay, ay.'

Sam   Yes, that's. Very good. Erm . . .

Ray   Yo why didn't you pick UKIP, aren't they gonna win?

Sam   Uh no, UKIP aren't going to 'win', and –

Shayne   Nah, you should have gone Labour, I'm telling you.

Michelle   Like you know anything, Shayne.

Shayne   Uh, I do actually, so –

Sam   I don't believe in the Labour Party's principles.

Muznah   My dad says that you're all the same, now. And that you're all shit.

Michelle   Muz!

Sam   No, don't worry, you can say what you like. I'm not a politician. That's the point. My job is to find the truth. It's why I'm here.

Michelle   So we ain't got to do music for a month, sir?

Sam   Please don't call me Sir. Did Mrs Gillon not explain why I was here?

Heather   A little bit.

Tommo   It's coz Mr Lucas has got Rabies, innit.

Sam   Your music teacher hasn't got Rabies. But he is away for a couple of weeks. So we hand picked you guys to help us out with a little project. It's actually quite a cool thing, you erm . . . well you get to have your voices heard and input into things that could one day become law. So . . .

Heather   What about our music GCSE, we gotta pass it, haven't we?

Sam   Well that's why you were chosen by Mrs Gillon, as students who are excelling and could afford to miss three or four lessons.

Shayne (*spurts laughter*)   Not Raymondo. He needs all the help he can get.

Ray   Fuck you!

Sam   Oy, come on now.

Michelle   It's true, Ray, you are pretty crump.

Ray   Yeah, laugh it up, cause one day you gonna be paying to see me spinning decks –

Shayne   Yeah right, you can't even play Frere Jacques.

Everyone laughs. **Ray** *heads over to the piano and sits at it.*

Ray   Yeah, all right, fuck you all! Watch this.

Sam   OK, come on everyone.

Ray   I'll show you Frere Jacques. I'm gonna Frere Jacques the fuck out of this.

(*Plays a note*) Wait.

(*Plays a couple of notes*) Wait.

(*Plays a note*) Wait.

(*Plays the first bit, goes wrong*) Wait.

Ray *plays* Frere Jacques *on the piano, clunkily, slowly, but gets through it. Slamming down on the keys, and standing victoriously.*

Ray   Yes! Recognise.

Sam   OK, well done. / Now. Can we –

Ray   Eat your heart out Stevie Fucking Wonder. (*Imitates Stevie Wonder on an air piano*).

Sam   All right, could we, like grab chairs and sit down please. Like . . . yeah in a circle, or . . .

The gang slovenly gather chairs and place them around, sitting.

Sam   Whatever. Cool. Thank you. So. Essentially. I'm here because, one, I'm interested in getting your opinions on a couple of matters, and, and two, because, as I'm sure you, you may or may not agree, that young people are often excluded from the political system or just, or feel disillusioned with the whole thing. More of you, when you reach voting age – you're like, what? Fifteen, sixteen?

Adam/ Tommo/ Michelle   Sixteen.

Ray/ Shayne/ Heather/ Muznah   Fifteen.

Sam   Right, so when you reach voting age, more of you will choose to vote in the X Factor than at the next general election.

Muznah   That's because what's the point, nothing changes.

Shayne   So what's your job then? What do you do?

Sam *goes to a flip chart and turns the sheet over. A drawing of a penis is there. The students burst into laughter, accusing and congratulating each other. They laugh into silence as they watch* **Sam**, *waiting to see what he'll say or do.*

Sam *smiles slightly, and nods, as he draws a line from the 'slit' of the penis drawing, all the way down, splitting it into left and right. He then begins to colour one side in red, half the other in blue, and the bottom half yellow.*

Sam   The House of Commons. The Government at the moment is a coalition of us and the Liberal Democrats Labour, because together we have more MPs in the Commons that any other party, including the opposition, Labour.

Shayne   Yeah, Labour, whoow whoow whoow.

Michelle   Ohmygod, seriously, Shayne.

Shayne   What?

Sam   And then other smaller parties here.

Ray   Yo, where's UKIP?

Sam   They don't have any.

Ray   They don't have any?

Sam   No, not yet –

Tommo   What about BNP.

Muznah   Tommo.

Tommo   That was a serious question.

Sam   It's all right. Again, they don't have any yet. So, MPs from the government side, here, they form a cabinet with each of them taking on different departments, whether it be 'Health' (*Writing, and so on*), 'Defence', 'Schools', 'Culture' and so on. I research for the Schools Secretary.

Adam   What do you research?

Ray (*mock-gay*) 'What do you research'.

Sam Hey. Please. So, um . . . so at this point in time, the government is producing a pretty far-reaching Schools Bill with things that will affect if not you then those slightly younger than you, their daily lives. Do you know what a Bill is?

Muznah Not like a phone bill?

Ray Idiot.

Muznah I / was joking, dick head,

Sam When ministers are formulating policies they'll normally submit a 'Green Paper' –

Michelle What's that?

Sam It's like a first draft of ideas. Then they get feedback from people within the industry in question, so like schools, hospitals, whatever, and then redraft the Green Paper into a White Paper. More consultation, until finally the minister in question will submit a 'Bill' to the House.

Ray Not a phone bill, Muz.

Muznah One more time! I / was fucking joking, cock nose!

Sam A Bill . . . OK, a bill is a possible future law, but before the MPs can vote we go into committee stage. That's what we're in now. This is where the MPs from other parties can try and make changes to the our proposed Bill. The idea being we all try and get the law as near perfect as possible before we all vote. If more MPs vote for it to become an Act of Parliament than not, then it becomes law. So –

Tommo Sir, did you vote for the Iraq war?

Sam I'm not a Member of Parliament, I'm just a member of the public. And please call me Sam. What I want to find out about is what *you* think to some of the things we're debating in this Bill. Lowering the voting age for you guys, reorganising the curriculum. Things such as raising the school leaving age –

Muznah What?!

Sam   So I was thinking we could form our own cabinet, if you like. To debate ideas. Like the real one. We each take a role. So someone will need to be Prime Minister –

Ray   I will!

Michelle   No way.

Sam   Which we'll vote on. Someone to be Environment, Transport, so on. And see how we go.

Ray   Michelle, why not me?

Heather   I think Tommo.

Shayne   No, he needs to be Defence, so he can protect us from Trip. (*Laughs*).

Michelle   Is culture like dance and sport and all that? That's the one I want.

Sam   OK, so. Next week, why not come prepared with your top two preferred positions, uh, and we'll vote. Or something.

Heather   Are we gonna get like a certificate for this or something?

Sam   Well, you'll get to contribute to Conservative Party policy.

Heather   Yeah, I want a certificate.

Tommo (*to* **Shayne**)   Oy, get the fuck out of my bag!

Shayne   I need a pen, knob rash!

Tommo *tries to snatch his rucksack back, and* **Shayne** *stands, holding it out tauntingly.* **Shayne** *goes to get it, and a chase ensues, with the others leaping to their feet and running round in a circle after* **Tommo**; **Sam** *trying to control them. The classroom fades as the shouts of the students turn into a nursery rhyme. They change clothes, taking off blazers, turning jumpers inside out etc.* **Adam** *becomes* **Young Teddy**; **Shayne** *becomes* **Young John**; *the rest become* **Kids**. **Sam** *watches, before disappearing . . .*

Broadstairs, 1920s.

Kids (*singing*)   'The farmer wants a wife; the farmer wants a wife,

Heigh-ho, Benjioh, the farmer wants a wife.

(*The **Kid** playing the farmer picks a wife*).

The wife wants a child; the wife wants a child,

Heigh-ho, Benjioh, the wife wants a child.

(*The **Kid** playing the wife picks a child*).

The child wants a dog; the child wants a dog,

Heigh-ho, Benjioh, the child wants a dog.

(*The **Kid** playing the nurse picks a dog*).

The dog wants a bone; the dog wants a bone,

Heigh-ho, Benjioh, the dog wants a bone.

(*The **Kid** playing the dog picks **Young Teddy**, and everyone starts patting him*).

We all pat the bone; we all pat the bone,

Heigh-ho, Benjioh, we all pat the bone!

*The kids pat **Young Teddy** to the ground until he struggles free.*

Young Teddy   Ouch! Get off! John, tell them.

Kid   Look, over there!

Kid   An empty dinghy!

Kid   It must have floated away!

Young John   Come on, then, let's grab it.

Kid   Let's sail to France!

Kids   Yeah!

The **kids** *exit cheering.* **Young Teddy** *follows but* **Young John** *pulls him back.*

Young John   Teddy, you've got to stay here.

Young Teddy   What? Why?

Young John   They're *my* friends, and they don't even like you, and you don't even like them anyway. And you wouldn't like the way we play, so . . .

Young Teddy   Yes I would, why wouldn't I like it?

Young John   'Cause you get wet, and you hate getting wet, and you get dirty, and you hate getting dirty, and you have to be a boy or a girl that's a bit like a boy, and you're just a girl so (*Blows a raspberry*).

Mrs Heath (*calling, off*)   Edward!

Mrs Heath *enters.*

Mrs Heath   What are you boys playing?

Young John   Mum, can I go and get in a dinghy with my friends?

Mrs Heath   Yes, of course, John. Run along.

Young Teddy   Can I, Mother?

Mrs Heath   Teddy, why would you want to go and do a thing like that?

Young John   See.

Young John *runs off, scruffy and dirty, as* **Young Teddy** *gets fixed by* **Mrs Heath***, clothes straightened and face wiped etc.*

Mrs Heath   Now Teddy, you know you've your lesson with Miss Locke. Don't you want to learn?

Young Teddy   I know, mother. I do want to learn, honestly.

Young Kay *returns to fetch a hat. She looks at* **Young Teddy***, giggles, and exits.*

Mrs Heath   One of your friends, hmm?

Young Teddy   No, I don't . . . I don't even know her name.

Mrs Heath   It's Kay, Teddy. You know that. (*Sighs, wipes him down*). You're ever such a bright boy, Teddy. Such a bright little boy. I'd hate you to get . . . distracted with . . .

Young Teddy   I won't. Mother. I promise.

Mrs Heath (*looks at him. Smiles. Stands*)   Good.

Miss Locke *appears by the piano.* **Mrs Heath** *holds* **Young Teddy's** *hand.*

Mrs Heath   Busy morning on the stall, Miss Locke?

Miss Locke   Yes, Mrs Heath, very busy.

Mrs Heath   What have they been going for today, I wonder?

Miss Locke   Geraniums today, Mrs Heath. We've had a run on them.

Mrs Heath   Geraniums? Isn't it funny? From one day to the next. Geraniums, you say?

Miss Locke   Hot cakes, Mrs Heath. Like hot cakes, I swear.

Mrs Heath   Well there you are. Geraniums, Teddy.

Miss Locke   Hello Teddy.

Mrs Heath   Say hello to Miss Locke, Teddy. He's been ever so keen to get started.

Miss Locke   I hope so.

Mrs Heath   Haven't you?

Little Teddy   Yes.

Mrs Heath   Ever so keen.

Miss Locke   Are you, Teddy?

Little Teddy   Yes.

Mrs Heath   Yes, ever so keen. (*Beat*). Jolly good, well I'll be through here.

Mrs Heath *exits. Silence.* **Miss Locke** *wanders around, occasionally turning to look at* **Young Teddy** *and smile, until eventually just stopping and smiling at him.*

Miss Locke   Such a terribly serious boy, Teddy. You've always struck me as being a Terribly, terribly serious. boy; don't you ever have any fun? (*Pause*). Why don't you ever smile Teddy; don't you ever smile?

Young Teddy (*smiles*).

Miss Locke   That isn't a smile, Teddy; that's a terrible smile.

Young Teddy (*frowns*).

Miss Locke   And that's a frown; what you're doing now, Teddy. That isn't a smile. (*Gasps*). Look at that, that's one of the biggest frowns I think I've ever seen. You know, if you turned that frown the other way around, it would be the biggest smile I've ever seen. Don't you want to turn it upside down, Teddy. Like this.

Miss Locke *turns around and bends over, one hand on the floor, lifting her dress with the other and looking at* **Young Teddy** *through her legs.*

Miss Locke   As though you were about to stand on your head, Teddy. Turn upside down like this.

Young Teddy (*suspiciously turns round and bends over, looking at her through his legs*).

Miss Locke   There you go. That frown's a smile now, Teddy. You've got a lovely smile.

They stay like this for some time. **Miss Locke** *stands.*

Miss Locke   Well I hope you're serious about learning to play the piano, Teddy, because quite honestly I haven't the time to ruddy waste, do you understand?

Young Teddy (*nods*).

Miss Locke   Well let's get started then.

Miss Locke *goes and sits at the piano. Pats the seat.* **Young Teddy** *joins her.*

Miss Locke   Now. I'm going to teach you scales and I'm going to show you arpeggios and I want you to practice them every day. And I'll know, you know. I'll be able to tell if you haven't practiced every single day. OK?

Young Teddy (*nods*).

Miss Locke   Very good, Teddy. Very good.

Miss Locke *plays.* **Sam** *appears, away from this, sat crossed leg, reading a book. He turns the page as* **Miss Locke** *fades, and* **Young Kay** *appears, playing hospital. She has a stethoscope.* **Young Teddy** *joins her on the floor.*

Young Kay   Come on, Teddy. I need to check your heart beat. (*Lifting his shirt*).

Young Teddy (*yelping*)   Kay! It's cold.

Young Kay   Look. Do you want to die? Because you will if I don't give you a check up.

Young Teddy   No.

Young Kay (*packing away*)   Fine. Go out and play with your friends then.

Young Teddy   You're my friend.

Young Kay   What?

Young Teddy (*beat. Shrugs*)   You know. (You're my . . .) . . .

Young Kay *smiles, and puts the stethoscope on his chest again. They burst into giggly hysterics, clambering over each other in a play fight. They stop,* **Young Kay** *on top of* **Young Teddy**.

Young Kay   One day, we're going to get married you know.

Young Teddy (*scrambling free*)   Urgh, I don't think so.

Young Kay   Our mothers think so. I just heard them talking in the kitchen. You have to ask me, though. The boy always asks the girl.

Young Teddy (*putting on the nurse's hat*)   Why?

Young Kay   I don't know but that's just the way it is. I have to wait. And you have to ask.

Young Teddy (*beat. As a female nurse*)   'Now young Lady. I am your nurse, Tedweena. And I need to check your heart beat. So lie down for me, there's a good girl.'

Young Kay *lies down as* **Young Teddy** *tickles her with the stethoscope on her stomach, as they laugh and fight some more.* **Sam** *closes his book and steps into:*

Sam's Office. Houses of Parliament.

Evening. **Sam** *is by the entrance facing* **James***, as though he's just got back.*

Sam   I'm sorry, who did?

James   I'm sorry?

Sam   Who let you in?

James   She did. Uh, the girl. She said just wait in here.

Sam (*beat. Goes to his desk, dumping his things*)   Sorry, I . . . sorry, I just wasn't – I thought we said we'd meet downstairs.

James   Did we? Oh. Everything all right, though?

Sam   Uhuh. Yep. Sorry. Busy day. (*Busying himself*). How, how's everything over at, uh . . . at Labour HQ?

James   Oh you know. Same same. How about you? Still buggering up our schools legacy? Ha.

Sam   Uh well, it was pretty shit legacy actually, so –

James   Not my lot, I've nothing to do with it. / And I was only joking.

Sam   No, you know, but . . . you know. Your side.

James   Right. (*Pause*). Still got stuff to do?

Sam   Uh, I've, I'm in the, uh . . . the press office tonight, so . . .

James   You're . . .? Sorry, you're . . . working tonight?

Sam   Later. Yes.

James   Oh. Oh. Sorry, are . . . are we not . . .? Going out?

Sam   Uh, yeah. If you . . . for like a . . . drink.

James   But . . . (*Looks at his watch. Beat*). Right. So *one* drink.

Sam   Yes.

James   Oh.

Sam   Is that . . .?

James   I just . . . I suppose because it was tonight, I had it in my head we were off to the, you know, the drinks. And then . . .

Sam   Oh. No, I . . . no, I never really . . . do all that.

James   No, I don't see you around, actually. You're not someone who I see around.

Sam (*smiles, politely. Continues busily*).

James   Are you . . .? Yeah, someone was saying, you've got some . . . (*Laughs*), um, little. Project on or something? Using school children as witnesses to the Bill. That's . . . was that yours? Great gimmick, if it was. Well done.

Sam   Asking school children what school children want for their schools is a gimmick?

James   Well. Yeah. (*Beat. Takes out a note*). I'm sorry, you did give me your number didn't you? That was you? 'Call me, 0–2–0 . . .' etcetera etcetera.

Sam (*stops. Looks at him. Beat*)   Um. Do you . . . actually, sorry, do you know what . . .

James   No, that's fine.

Sam   I'm just not . . . now is a bad time, sorry. I'm . . . not ready . . .

James   Well. Maybe let's try next week. Uh?

Sam   Yeah, sure, Give, give . . . drop me a . . .

James (*leaving the note on the desk opposite and nodding*)   Cool.

Broadstairs, 1930s.

Teenage Teddy *appears at the piano with* **Miss Locke***, playing together.*

Miss Locke   Very good, Teddy. I'm ever so proud, you know. Would you like me to continue coming round? Now that you're 'proficient'?

Teenage Teddy (*pause. Shrugs*).

Miss Locke   Only I've plenty other things that need doing. If you don't need me anymore. (*Pause*). I've a boyfriend now, you know. He's ever such a dish. Do you have a girlfriend, Teddy? (*Pause*). What about that Kay, girl, hmm? I won't tell your mother, I swear it. Cross my heart and hope to die. (*Pause*). You know, you really shouldn't spend so much time with your mother. (*Pause*). Teddy?

Miss Locke *leans in and kisses him on the cheek. He doesn't move.*

Miss Locke   What do you make of that, hmm? How did that make you feel?

Teenage Teddy (*pause. Shrugs*).

Miss Locke   Very well, Teddy. (*Stands*). Very well. (*Exits*).

House of Commons Library.

Douglas *at work.* **Sam** *enters.*

Douglas   Ah, morning morning. (*Indicating a pile*). Here we are, ready and waiting.

Sam   Uh. Thanks. Actually, I was wondering if I could . . .
(*handing over a list*) . . . if you could maybe dredge up anything in
addition to . . . your 'present'. Yesterday.

Douglas   Um. Okay Cokey. But, uh . . . (*looking at the list*),
you won't find anything, you know . . . 'revelatory'. If there was
something, it would be out by now. Believe me.

Sam   Well I don't even know what I'm looking for, so . . . I know
there'll be no, uh, 'lines' written down, but I at least want to *see* the
lines that are, so that I may . . . read in between them. If you see
my . . . (point).

Douglas   Of course. (*Makes to leave. Stops*). I did meet him once,
you know? I was here on work experience, years ago. He was the
Father the House, then. Longest serving MP. My Granddad used to
say that the Father's haunt this place. Here for so long in life they
can't leave it. Even in death.

Sam (*smiles politely. Gestures the note*)   See what you can do.

Kay *and* **Teddy** *appear, dancing waltz in a light, the music
distorted and ephemeral. They disappear.*

Sam *watches from the side. He leaves, as the music dies . . .*

Broadstairs, 1940s.

Kay *and* **Teddy** *walking home.*

Kay   I love dances. You should have worn your uniform. These
military types can be so dapper and smart, I think. (*Beat*). What
was it like?

Teddy   What was what like?

Kay   The war. Being away. Fighting.

Teddy   Well. Can't say I really . . . you know, unlike some, really
. . . fought. But . . .

Kay *skips forward a little, walking back to face him.*

Kay   You really are quite a good dancer, you know.

Teddy   Oh. Not really. I was just following you, Kay.

Kay *takes his hands and leads him forward as they twirl round together.* **Ted** *makes a show of resisting, before relenting. And laughing. They carry on walking.*

Kay   Back to London for you, then, tomorrow? Any word on vacant seats?

Teddy   No, not yet. It's simply a matter of waiting. Job keeps me busy. You? How's the school?

Kay   Oh fine. You know. Boys will be boys.

Teddy (*stopping*)   Well here we are, then. (*Beat*). This is where we part.

Kay   Sorry?

Teddy (*indicating*)   This your road, isn't it?

Kay   Well. Yes, but –

Teddy   Ten minutes, you should be fine. I'm this way.

Kay   Uh. Yes, all . . . Gosh looks very muddy. Might even have to . . . (*Takes off one of her shoes*) . . . get rid of these. Don't want to twist an ankle.

Teddy   Okay dokey.

Kay (*beat. Nods to herself, taking off the other heel. Beat*)   You know, you're . . . don't – you're more than welcome to . . . see me all the way to my door, if you'd like.

Teddy   No, that's all right, thank you. My mother will probably be waiting up, anyway,

Kay   Right. Well. (*Waits expectantly. Small sigh. Kisses him on the cheek*). Goodbye, Ted.

Teddy   Cheerio.

Kay *hobbles off one way, and* **Teddy** *strolls of the other . . .*

Sam's Office.

Late. **Sam** *looking through books, lit by lamps.* **Nicholas** *enters slumping down at the other desk opposite, exclaiming dramatically.*

Nicholas   Why can't I escape!!

Sam   How'd it go?

Nicholas   Well. If they *did* offer me a job I wouldn't take it because I couldn't work for a company so stupid they'd employ me based on *that* interview. (*Buries his head*). Oh God. (*Looks at his watch*). 7pm, Sam. Why you still here? What you reading?

Sam (*closing the book*)   Nothing.

Nicholas   Oh-oh . . . (*As though talking to a child*). Sam's up to something, yes he is. I can always tell.

(*Off* **Sam's** *look*). Oh Sam. Sam-Sam. Why are you still here?

Sam   I'm just finishing up, I'll go / in a sec.

Nicholas   No, why are you *here?* I know why I'm here. I can't get a job combing old people's hair. But you. Michael has said he will recommend you for anything. I'll . . . recommend you. (*With letters from* **Sam's** *desk*). Look. Just sat here. His reference. My reference. You could climb three, four rungs up the ladder. All you have to say is where. So Why Are You Still Here?

Sam   I'm not . . . I don't – I'm not sure that *this* is the ladder I want to climb. The . . . this behind the scenes stuff, I think I actually . . . I don't, that I actually might . . .

Nicholas   Oh my God, I knew it. (*Indicating the adjoining office door*). You want to be one of them, don't you?

Sam   I . . . (*Shrugs*) . . . I, I don't . . . I'm not . . .

Nicholas   Hey, no listen. It's not like it wasn't obvious, even if it wasn't to you. All this . . . benevolent extracurricular stuff, like with the kids and shit. You're just, you're one of those that . . . you know. Want to. Make things better. I personally couldn't give a blind man's fuck and that's why I'm getting out. (*Beat*). Sam. A 'politician'. (*Smiles*). Ah, which now makes sense about the gay thing. I like your thinking.

Sam   What thing, what thinking?

Nicholas   You know. Keeping it on the down low. No parties, no . . . you know, no really 'gay' stuff.

Sam   I'm . . . I don't know what you mean. Sorry.

Nicholas   Well you know. Yes you do. Around here. On *this* ladder, it makes no difference. Does it? Diversity? Uh, 'yes.' But on that other ladder. Politics in public. Out there. (*Indicates window & 'real' world*). You know? It's different. You can't . . . 'flaunt it'.

Sam   Flaunt it?

Nicholas   OK. I see you're getting . . . I was, I'm just trying to help. I've been in this party longer, I know what it's like.

Sam   OK, I'm – then tell me, I'm listening.

Nicholas   No, you're being passive aggressive, that's not the / same as listening.

Sam   OK, I'm sorry –

Nicholas   And now you're interrupting. (*Pause*). Look, it's just about being sensible, isn't it, if this one thing that never changes in the Conservative Party, it's its propensity to completely and utterly fuck itself up over two things, no matter what else changes in the world, the two things we just can't bloody well get over – Europe, and gays. Whether it's 1983 or 2013, you want to freak out a Tory?, give him a croissant in one hand and a copy of Attitude in the other and he will literally pass out. It's the rope we like to hang ourself with, same for Thatcher, same for Major, same for your boy Heath – Christ, a gay man who took us into Europe?! (*Does the crucifix sign, hissing*). And it's the thing that's killing Cameron, too. You watch, nothing changes.

Sam   Why do you keep saying 'your boy'.

Nicholas   Not Like That – but he is, he's like a posher, older version of you, socially liberal, straddling the centre, nicer, greener – hey, great, fine, modern, lovely, me? I'm Totes in the Boris club, that big blonde bitch will get my vote every time. Which it will. And you'll still be kneeling at Cameron's altar, kissing his ring. Oop, matron.

Sam   Nicholas, we've just celebrated the wedding of two male Tory MPs, I'm just gonna put it out there that I think we might finally be getting over ourselves.

Nicholas   Yeah, here in the Westminster village, for shiz, absolutely, but there's a world of difference between the cosmopolitan London set who get voted in, and the CofE, blue rinse, Daily Mail readers who *vote* them in. I'm mean even those two, the 'Groom and Groom', they waited till they were near the top before they, like, 'announced', and that's all I'm saying to you. I'm saying they don't . . . you know, they're not 'really' gay.

Sam   They're not – what? They're not –

Nicholas   They covered their tracks, is all. There are no seedy stories, no pictures.

Sam   Why would there be seedy stories / just because they're –

Nicholas   I'm saying you'd make an excellent candidate, Sam!, just let your work do the talking, and if you shine, you can be whatever you want. You like men, women, old people, goats, hey. You might think the country has changed but it hasn't all that. And you might think the party's changed but you know that isn't true either. *We're* different, the new intake are different. The young 'uns. And the front bench is different. Hurrah. But behind them in the House and filling the hall of the conference are party members as rooted in the Right as they have ever been. And they will have a black, Islamic wheelchair bound Frenchman as Prime Minister before we see a fella kissing his other half on the steps of number 10. And you know I'm right. (*Pause*). Christ, I'm just saying if you want to climb that ladder, don't make it an issue.

Sam   I didn't! You did! What are you actually telling me to do, be less gay?

Nicholas   Is that what I said? / Is that what I said?!

Sam   I've no fucking clue what you're saying to be honest, Nicholas!

Nicholas   Don't you speak to me like that, I am still your fucking chief of staff! (*Pause*). All right? Jesus H. I'm saying keep on doing what you're doing, for Christ's sake! (*Pause*). Well now I'm in an even worse mood, thanks very fucking much.

Sam (*bangs the desk. Pause*)   I literally, I can't believe it's still . . .

Nicholas (*pause*)   Look, I didn't . . . things, they came out wrong, please don't . . . I'm – don't make this an . . . a thing. (*Pause*). Sam? We cool?

Sam (*nods his head*).

Nicholas *turns his desk lamp off – and that half of the room descends into darkness. He exits.* **Sam** *reads at his desk, lit by a lamp. His phone rings.*

Sam (*answers*)   Yes?

Ted *on the phone, flicks on a lamp at the desk opposite, holding* **James***'s note.*

Ted   Hello?

Sam   Hello. Who's that?

Ted (*looking at the note*)   Have I got the wrong number?

Sam *slams the phone down and stares at it.*

Ted's Office, House of Commons, 1950s.

Ted *is holding the phone, as before, looking confused at his note. He hangs up and stares out into the darkness.*

He picks the phone up again and redials, just as **Timothy** *and* **Frank** *enter slovenly and yawning, with cups of tea.* **Ted** *puts the phone down.*

Ted   Morning, Gentleman.

Frank   Well that's the understatement of the year, Mr Heath.

Ted   Lots to do, lots to do.

Timothy   You know, I never knew there was a six o'clock in the morning, Frank.

Frank   No?

Timothy   No. I knew there was one in the evening, I've seen it. Every day. Bang on at six o'clock. But I did not know until today that there was another one. In the morning.

Ted (*handing out lists*)   Frank. Tim.

Timothy   We were out late at that Kensington fundraiser, Mr Heath.

Ted   Your government needs you, Gentlemen, time to set to work, all right?

Frank   We were working last night, Mr Heath.

Ted   You were drinking last night.

Timothy   You can drink and work at the same time, that's what fundraisers are, drinking and working; working and drinking, my God I think I could sleep standing up. I do, I really do –

Frank (*reading*)   A Three-line Whip for a Transport and Denationalisation Bill. Makes me want to cry.

Timothy   The Chief could have mentioned it last night when we were necking our gins.

Ted   He didn't know himself then, this comes straight from the top.

Frank   Oh well thank you very much, Mr Churchill –

Ted   Look. (*Serious*). We are hanging on by a thread, do you understand? We are literally under attack in there every single day.

It's a barrage. And whether or not it's a Bill to regulate the size of grass or a Bill to invade Canada, the Opposition will divide the other way every single time. All it takes is a handful of our chaps to get a cold, sprain their ankle, or miss the bus, and we couldn't pass the parcel, let alone a law. So be good chaps and get to it. (*Dialling*).

Timothy   Five past six on a Monday morning. They're gonna be angry.

Ted   They are going to be loyal! Gentleman. (*Gesturing their phones*). If you please. (*On his phone*). Ah. Mrs Turnbull. Joint Deputy Whip, sorry to bother you so early in the morning. Could I just have a small word with your husband please?

He's where?

The House of Commons? (*Winces at* **Timothy** *and* **Frank**).

No, no. I'm sure you're right. We obviously just keep missing him. Apologies again.

Ted *puts the phone down and stares at* **Tim** *and* **Frank** *with a 'whoops' look.*

Ted   Uh, Tim, pull the card on Turnbull, would you? Stockton-on-Tees.

Tim *opens a drawer. Inside is a vast system of index cards. He flicks through them, until he finds the one he needs.*

Tim   Stockton. Got it.

Ted   Write on it. 'Marital problems' stop. Brackets 'adultery question mark'.

Frank   Well. When we bump into old tearaway Turnbull later I'm sure we won't have to worry which way he'll be voting, now will we?

Ted   The information we record is not for the purposes of blackmail, Frank, it is to foresee the potential for scandal and to nip it in the bud before it blossoms. Make sure we get him in this afternoon, will you? (*Small beat*). And incidentally, yes, make sure he does understand that he'll be voting with us.

Frank *salutes.* **Ted** *leaves with an empty cup in search of tea.*
Frank *whacks* **Tim** *with his list,* **Tim** *whacks* **Frank** *with his, as*
they slowly begin to work.

Tim Watch it.

Frank You watch it. How's your head?

Tim Like an elephant is sat on it. (*Looking at the cards*). God,
look at this. A litany of misadventures and sins. Very proud of
this system, he is. I don't care what he says, he loves the gossip.
(*Reading*). Adultery. Alcoholism. Sodomy. If it's wrong, I can
guarantee you that somewhere there is a Tory doing it. Awh. Look
at this. 'Edward Heath, Bexley'. Completely blank. That makes me
sad.

Frank (*dialling*) I'm quite proud of the few black marks against
my name, Tim.

Tim As am I, Frankie boy. As am I.

Frank Sign of a life lived, I always think.

Tim I entirely agree with you, Frank. I do entirely agree. But not
our Teddy here.

Ted *returns as* **Frank** *speaks on the phone:* **Ted** *and* **Tim**
continuing over.

Frank (*on the phone*) Morning, Mr Whitehouse? / How do
you do sir, Frank in the Whips Office. Just sounding our boys out
regarding the Transport bill for this evening. Patrick's adamant it's
a full house for this one. (*Pause*). Right . . . (*Continuing*).

Tim Did you have a nice weekend, then, Mr Heath? Get up to
any fun?

Ted Oh. You know. You?

Tim Oh yes, thank you very much, yes indeed sir. Met a lovely
young thing out in Southfields. A dance that my brother helped
organised. Lovely she was. You?

Ted Oh. The usual.

Tim   And what's that then?

Ted   Sorry?

Tim   What's the usual, Mr Heath?

Ted   You know. Quiet weekend.

Tim   Go out anywhere? Meet anyone? Do anything?

Ted   Are you making your way through that list all right, Timothy? Time is ticking.

Frank (*putting the phone down*)   I am. Aldershot confirmed. (*Picking up the phone*). Right, Altringham.

Tim   I was just asking Mr Heath what he got up to over the weekend, Frank.

Frank   Oh, and what did he get up to, Tim, anything?

Tim   I'm just trying to find that out, Frank. Mr Heath? Anything?

Ted *whips a baton out of his pocket, spins round, and begins. Music.* **Tim** *and* **Frank** *freeze. As* **Ted** *waves his stick, almost like a magic wand,* **Tim** *and* **Frank** *follow, reversing out of the office, as it begins to fade into the music classroom.*

Music Classroom.

Ray, **Tommo**, **Michelle**, **Adam**, **Muznah**, **Shayne** *and* **Heather** *sat in a semicircle with notes and papers.* **Sam** *pacing, distracted . . .*

Michelle   So as Education Secretary, right, it is my recommendation that we don't change the school leaving age to eighteen, based on the fact that school and academics and all that, yeah, is not for every pupil, and it would be better for those for which it ain't to go out and get jobs and start earning. (*Beat*). Sir?

Sam   Uh, sorry. Right. Yes. OK. Um. So you plan to basically keep things as they are?

Michelle   Ba-sic-a-lly, yeah . . .

Sam   Thoughts, Prime Minister?

Adam   I agree. I think we're old enough to make our own choices.

Sam   But what about skills? That means these guys and girls are leaving untrained.

Michelle   Train on the job, though. Won't learn to build a building in the classroom.

Sam   What about crime. Home secretary?

Tommo (*pause*)   Is that me?

Ray (*laughs*).

Sam   Surely keeping kids busy in school or on apprenticeships gives them aspirations, gives them hope. Education plays a very important social role.

Shayne   We aren't all criminals, sir.

Michelle   Well just give 'em more stuff to do, yeah. Youth centres and stuff.

Tommo   And more police. Kick 'em in line, innit.

Sam   So you're going to spend money on police for when they *are* criminals rather than in education *before* they get the chance? OK. Gonna need to raise taxes, Chancellor.

Shayne   Fine, I'll raise taxes.

Adam   No. We're not.

Shayne   Fuck off, it's my call.

Adam   Sir, is the Chancellor really allowed to tell the Prime Minister to fuck off?

Sam   No. Well. The last one used to, but anyway. If you want to raise taxes (*Sucking in air*) that means families are going struggle more, perhaps leading to an *increase* in crime. When you've just invested all this money in extra police. How can that be?

Shayne (*sighs*)   I don't know, sir.

The school bell. They stand and begin to pack away/ get ready to leave.

Sam   Well. It's something to think about for next time.

Heather   Well why don't you just tell us the right answer, sir?

Sam   There is no necessarily 'right' answer, that's the point.

Muznah   He'd raise taxes. My dad says all they're ever after is our money.

Sam   Not at all. We believe in low taxes. In fact one of the traditional divides between Labour and Tory, (*Indicates two separate groups that have formed as the students pack away*), Left and Right, socialism and capitalism or whatever is just that.

Ray (*running over to the other 'Tory' group*)   Fuck, I'm voting Conservative then.

Sam   Well, it just depends where you stand. Both arguments are good ones.

Muznah   How can high taxes ever be good, it ain't fair, man,

Sam   Well Labour traditionally seek higher taxes because they believe in higher spending, and that if we all chuck in to the pot, then we all benefit. Problem is that means the tax burden on families is high. Conservatives believe if taxes are lower, the individual, men, women and families are able to succeed on their own terms, they move everyone forward with them. But it's difficult. It is. I've grappled with it. This country has always grappled with it, flipping from one side to the other. In the seventies, more Left; in the eighties, more Right. And that's what you need to decide. Your party, your government. Which way. Welcome to power.

Michelle   Sir? What if you don't believe your party has chosen the right way on something, do you still have to vote with them and stuff?

Sam   It's expected you will, yes. There's something called a Whip's office to check you do.

Michelle   But you just said you believed in individual choice. How is that fair?

Sam (*beat*)   I don't know.

Shayne   Bye, sir!

Ray   'Bye sir'! Gay. (*Feeling* **Adam***'s arse*).

Adam   Oy! The fuck you doing?! Why / you always doing that?

Sam   Hey! OK, everyone else, off you go. Ray. Wait here.

Ray   What? Fucking hell.

The others leave. **Sam** *is packing away his things.*

Sam   What's your issue with Adam; why do you go around calling him gay? Everyone gay?

Ray   Coz it's funny?

Sam   Well, when you get a little older you'll realise sexual preference, just like race, isn't something you should be insulted with.

Ray   I know that, yeah, it's just . . . when you say 'gay' you ain't saying, like '*gay*' gay, you're just saying, like . . . 'Uh, that's gay'. As in. A bit shit.

Sam   Some of the people you call gay might actually be gay and you're not helping them.

Ray   Yeah, I'm encouraging them to come out, innit. Why you so bothered? Are you gay, sir? (*Pause*). Are you? (*Pause. Smiles*). I won't tell anyone.

Sam   I'll see you next week Ray.

Sam's Office.

Evening. **Sam** *is at his desk.* **James** *stands facing him.*

Sam   I'm sorry.

James   I've been down there twenty minutes.

Sam   Time just slipped / away from me, I –

James   Like I was down there twenty minutes on Monday.
Getting a bit silly, now, isn't it?

Sam   I know, I'm not . . . it isn't / that I –

James   You do know people, don't you? You have interacted with
people before? Socially. You've not been . . . I don't know, in a
cave somewhere for twenty years. You've had, do have, friends.
Relationships. You are gay, aren't you Sam?

Sam   I've just been very . . . I'm not – and someone . . . said /
something to me that –

James   What are you finding so difficult about this? Are you . . .
what, ashamed or something?

Sam   And what have I got to be ashamed about?

James   I don't know, you tell me. You're an enigma, Sam.
Everything about you, maybe that's why I keep coming back.

Sam   Well I'm glad I can entertain you.

James   How did you pick this side?

Sam   Why shouldn't I pick this side.

James   Uh, I don't know, Northern, working class, gay, it's like
you were born with a labour badge on you.

Sam   Ah I see, right, Scouse accent, must be working class, that's
very open-minded of you, well done.

James   Fine but your home town, its background. Manufacture,
industry, all that. Industries and communities that your lot
destroyed when last in power, I'm just wondering your family,
your neighbours think about your choice of –

Sam   No, I agree, my hometown *is* no longer full of factories and
mines and quarries and mills, it is now full of business parks, and
retailers, and offices –

James   Well, gain a business park, lose a community. It's all
about balance.

Sam   Ah, yes, those mythical communities you like to pretend existed. Where nobody locked their doors and everyone knew their neighbours –

James   Oh is *that* why you picked this lot, I get it, yeah, 'independence', 'no society', not having to rely on, or trust, or get close to 'other people' –

Sam   Yeah what monsters we were, getting rid of dangerous industries and replacing them with good 9-to-5 jobs and consumers choices and lower taxes –

James   Ah yes. Money. 'The most important thing.' (*Smiles. Pause*). Shall I try again? In a few days? Just to see 'where you're at'? One last time?

Sam *shrugs.* **James** *shrugs back. Pause. He approaches* **Sam***, who moves back away from him, until his back hits the adjoining office door.* **James** *is close . . .*

James   What are you so scared of, Sam? I'm not scary. What is it . . .?

James *moves in for a kiss.* **Sam** *pushes past him and leaves.*

Sam   Wait, sorry I . . . just need a . . . glass of . . . (*exit*).

James *sighs. Pause. The door to the adjoining office opens, as* **Nicholas** *pops his head round to check the coast is clear. Seeing nothing, he opens the door fully out, hiding* **James** *behind it. He enters, closing the door to reveal* **James***.*

Nicholas   Oh. Hi.

James   Hi. You're. .?

Nicholas   Nicholas. You're . . . in my office.

James   You've been next door? In there?

Nicholas   Working late. You know.

Sam *comes back in.*

Sam   So, listen, uh . . . let's – (*sees* **Nicholas**). Hi.

Nicholas   Hello Sam.

Sam   This is James. He works over at, um . . . have you – you're popping in or . . .?

James   No, he was –

Nicholas   Yes. Yes, I've just popped in now. Just arrived.

James   Well, I was just heading off. So. (*Pause*). Bye.

James *exits. Silence.*

Sam   I'll be heading off as well then, Nick. See you tomorrow. (*Exiting*).

Nicholas   Bye bye now.

Ted *appears at the piano, playing.* **Mrs Heath** *is in a chair, a blanket over her, eyes closed.* **Sam** *watches . . .*

Ted *looks at his mother and stops playing. Long pause. He reaches his hand over and touches hers. He flinches back. She doesn't move. He reaches out and touches her again, holding her wrist. Nothing.* **Ted** *turns back to the piano. Beat. He plays.*

Library.

Sam *is with* **Douglas***, going through some books and old files –* **Sam** *is somewhat erratic throughout: pacing, leafing through things, tossing them aside . . .*

Sam   Where did you get all this?

Douglas   Easy if you know where to look. Most people don't look, that's all.

Sam   I can't believe it. This one – even communist spies tried to out him?!

Douglas   Well, *blackmail* him.

Sam   It, it, it's like – it's persecution, basically, it's –

Douglas   Wasn't unique to him, though, I could pull you a whole stack microfiches, declassified files showing how the Soviets looked for rising political stars they might be able to turn. I don't mean like that, I mean lure to the other side. Not like that I mean; I mean –

Sam   I know what you mean.

Douglas   With poor Mr. Heath, he was a lover of music –

Sam   I know, he played the organ at Christ Church – no, Balliol. One of them –

Douglas   And so the plan was to have this young male Czech organist come to London and 'bump into' young Ted. This lad would invite him over to Prague under the pretence of showing him his organ – uh so to speak. He'd then seduce him, bit of you know what – a gay honeytrap I believe would be the parlance *du jour* – and then they'd blackmail him afterwards. MI5 caught wind first, and warned Ted off.

Sam   So it must be true. MI5.

Douglas   Hard to say.

Sam   Why is it so hard to say?! Jesus. Don't give me rumours, gossip, bitching. There must be facts, doesn't anyone care about them anymore? What about the cottaging stuff? The police who told him to jack it in for his career – did they caution him, interview him? A former Prime Minister who had sex with men in toilets at a time when it was illegal to be gay, and not one bit of actual concrete proof?!

Douglas   Only what people say. But if more than one person says it . . . in my experience, then . . .

Sam   It's not good enough.

Douglas   What exactly are you hoping to find, Sam? And – why?

Sam   Right, so he must have been, then. If that's what fuckin – 'scuse me –

Douglas   You're excused –

Sam   – if that's what cold war spies tried to trap him with, he must have been gay.

Douglas   Well, rather intriguingly, I've got sources saying the plot was invented by right wing Conservatives who wanted to topple him as leader in favour of Mrs T. Which worked, incidentally.

Sam   And she's another one. Right? She told that news editor, *she* thought he was gay, whispering in corners with the others . . .

Douglas   Might I be so bold as to ask . . . why it matters?

Sam   Because it obviously *does* matter, doesn't it, still. Whether it was true or not, it's what they tried to bring him down with, time after time after time, I mean how do I – how did *he* stand a chance?

Douglas   Look, Sam. Look at what you're holding. (*Gesturing at the stuff in his hands*).

They're covered in dust. They're *old*. We're not there any more.

Sam (*gathering his things*)   We are if we choose to be.

Douglas   So don't choose to be. Let the past be the past.

Beat. **Sam** *grabs his stuff, leaves, stepping into:*

Sam's Office.

Nicholas *is on the phone as* **Sam** *enters, a bit annoyed* **Nicholas** *is in the office. He dumps his things on his desk and sits, working instantly.*

Nicholas   Very well, thank you, very well indeed. I got a message to call back.

Really? Well that's . . . oh my God, wow, I'm . . . I'm delighted, thank you so much, I don't know what to say. Huh . . .

Will do, no problem. OK. Thank you. Talk to you soon. Bye.

Nicholas *puts the phone down and leaps up, punch the air.*

Nicholas   Whoow! Yeah! Get in! Come on! You will never guess what Sammy-boy. I have been put on the candidate list to be (*Drum roll*) . . . bam bam bah! A Conservative councillor for Wandsworth. Courtesy of the local Putney Association. Booyakasha!

Sam   You . . . when . . . you applied to be a councillor? Why didn't you tell me?

Nicholas   Well, case I didn't get it.

Sam   I thought that kind of thing didn't . . . that you didn't care / about . . .

Nicholas   Yeah, well, You know, these councillors, great offers and shit, jobs, all that. What with their connections. Whoow! And, ey, as a fellow Wandsworth resident, I trust I have your vote.

Sits. Spins. Swivels. Laughs. Looks at **Sam**, *and sighs contentedly.*

Nicholas   Now. I know something that I know you don't know that I know about you.

Sam   What?

Nicholas   You know the other night. In here. When you came in. And I was with that boy. I hadn't just arrived. I'd been in Michael Two's office. Working late. So I know he hadn't just 'swung by'. Do you see? (*Pause*). Who does your boyfriend work for? He's not one of ours.

Sam   Well now I'm confused. For you see I do not have a boyfriend, so I cannot tell you for whom he works, do you see?

Nicholas   Hmm. ('Do you see'). Well, I knew you batted for the other side, Sam. I just didn't know you were batting *with* the other team. Blue and yellow is one thing but blue and red . . . awh, it makes 'pink', now it makes sense.

Sam   What?!

Nicholas   If I find out that you've been sneaking signals over the top to the other side –

Sam   How dare you -!

Nicholas (*bangs the desk*)   Do not interrupt me and don't presume to tell me / what I –

Sam (*standing, overlapping*)   I won't stay to listen to this.

Nicholas   – dare or dare not say. (*Standing*). Oh yes you fucking will, sit down.

Sam   How dare you –

Nicholas   There's Those Words Again. I / won't tell anyone but –

Sam   There's no rules saying you can't have . . . between – and / anyway I'm not fucking –

Nicholas   But I will tell you this. You're on a timer with me now, boyo. So I don't want any fuss, any accusations about things you think I may or may not have said during our little chat the other day. I don't want any threats; I basically just don't want you around. We don't like each other. Sam. Do we? If we're honest? Or at least I don't think you like me and I can't Stand people who don't like me. You've got your references. Get a position somewhere else. And leave. Make it soon, make it quiet, but make it quick. (*Pause*). Would you like me to go over anything?

Sam   . . . no . . .

Nicholas (*smiles, rubbing his hair, over-friendly*)   Then get outta here. You big queen.

Long pause, **Nicholas** *holding and smiling at* **Sam**. **Nina** *enters and they break.*

Nicholas   Nina, hey, guess what? Sam's decided he's moving on.

Nina   Oh. Cool. So you've finally chosen where you wanna go?

Nicholas   Catch you lovers later. (*Exits*).

Nina (*pause*)   You all right?

Sam (*nods, unconvincingly*).

Nina You sure?

The phone rings. **Sam** *answers.* **Ted** *appears, on the phone, holding the note.*

Sam Hello?

Ted Hello? Who's this?

Sam *slams the phone down and pushes away from the desk.* **Ted** *disappears.*

Sam Did you hear that?!

Nina What?

Sam That phone! Did it ring?

Nina Yes! Sam, what's wrong, are you OK?

Sam (*sitting. Pause. Tries to laugh, unconvincingly*). (*Pause*) Nina. What . . . what do people think of . . . am I . . .? Of me. What do . . .?

Nina Right now, I'm not sure. (*Smiles*). Kidding.

Sam No, but . . . am I – do people. Am I someone that it's. Quite hard to like . . .

Nina Sam, of course not. No . . .

Sam (God). Why these? Ey? This lot. This side of the fence. Why did you pick these?

Nina Blue brings out my eyes. (*Smiles. Beat*). I dunno. I remember at Uni, sharing a house. We'd have arguments about the washing up. I would just do mine. Another housemate would sometimes do other people's. Her point being if everyone chipped in, it's nicer. And fairer. I thought if everyone just did their own, it would always get done. I think that's when I knew. Or started to.

Sam (*pause. Half smile. Nods. Stands*) I . . . I have to . . . get to class . . .

Sam *saunters out.* **Nina** *follows.*

Hampstead Heath, 1950s. *A bright summer's day.*

Kay *is sat on one of two swings hanging from a tree.* **Ted** *stands. Watching her.*

Kay   You used to push me for hours at a time. Too high. I thought I'd go over the top.

Ted (*smiles*)   Hello, Kay.

Kay   Hello Ted. It's been a long time. I'm . . . awfully sorry about your mother.

Ted   Thank you for your card.

Kay   I meant to telephone but . . . life takes up so much time these days. Still, thanks for *your* call. I just adore Hampstead Heath in the summer. You come here often?

Ted   Um. Now and again, yes.

Kay   You must struggle to find the time. I hear you're doing terribly well.

Ted   They're considering me as a replacement for Sir Henry as full Deputy Whip.

Kay   Wow. Well, Teddy, that's wonderful. You really are / on the rise –

Ted   Only 'considering', though. They have . . . there are concerns.

Kay   Concerns, surely not. What concerns?

Ted   There are . . . rumours. (Not completely unsub–) . . . Problem, uh . . . (*Laughs, semi-tragically*), problem is, the rumours are all I have. In a void that other people fill with . . . I don't know what other people fill it with. 'A private life', I suppose. If the rumours disappears there's just a, a hole where . . .

Kay   Ted, are you all right?

Ted   I miss her. So much. I . . . have a, a . . . *pain* . . . here. And I need it to go. I need it to be . . . replaced. You wouldn't . . . believe some of the things I've been . . . trying to –

Kay (*stands*)   Oh Ted . . .

Ted *stumbles back with his hands up, not wanting to be touched.*
Kay *stops. He slumps down on the ground.*

Kay   Talk to me, Ted. Please. Why did you . . . is there a reason
you got back in touch?

Ted   A reason? (A reason . . . ah yes). And the orchestra
cease playing, the hall goes quiet, and all assembled are
awaiting my cadenza. If you'll allow me a moment to prepare.
(*He shifts. Looks at the earth beneath him*). London clay,
Hampstead Heath. Only really to be found in the south, you
know. Tough stuff. Contains some pretty amazing fossils by
all accounts, and crystals too, if one had only the inclination to
dig. (*Pause. Chuckles, tragically*). 'Heath'. Rambling. Desolate.
Low level plant life. Shrubbery and weeds. Can only grow so
high, before its inferior nature causes it to be surpassed by
those . . . stronger. A waste land. A waste space, waste *of* space,
just . . . (*Trails*).

I always thought if I was ever going to marry, Kay, then it would
be you. (*Short pause*). If I ever was, that is. But alas . . . that boat
has left the harbour. And I'm characteristically left standing alone
on the dock.

Kay   A girl can only wait so long. Teddy.

Ted (*nods*)   How is Richard?

Kay   He's fine. Thank you. We're both happy. And fine.

Ted   I'm sorry, Kay. I don't know what I was thinking.

Kay   Do you remember that Summer ball, Ted? I was going to
kiss you that night. Only you never found out because you said
goodbye and. . . Not out of . . . it was simply that . . . (*Sighs*).
Truth is, Ted, you're not like other people. In that you don't need
Other People. Not the way other people do. (*Beat*). We all make
sacrifices. You just have to make sure they're worth it.

Ted   I still have that photograph. By my bed. To remember
you.

Kay   I think the fact that you need a photograph, Ted . . . I think, speaks volumes. (*Smiles warmly*). Now stop sitting there all glum, and come play with me on the swings.

Beat. **Ted** *saunters over to the empty swing and sits. They start to swing together.*

Music Classroom.

Shayne, Tommo, Heather *and* **Muznah** *are dancing around to music from the CD player, while* **Adam, Ray** *and* **Michelle** *sit scribbling notes –* **Ray** *standing to contribute his own moves occasionally.* **Sam** *enters.* **Tommo** *presses stop.*

Tommo   Oh-oh. That's detention for you, sir.

Sam   Sorry, I'm . . . so sorry for being late, I got held up, and . . .

Michelle   We've nearly finished our Green Paper, sir.

Tommo *turns the music on again and dances, turning it off when* **Sam** *shouts.*

Sam   Cool. Uh, let me take a . . . (*to* **Shayne**). Could you . . . turn that off, please?!

Tommo   Why, we've done our paper, gotta get back into the music groove, you get me?

Michelle   This is more important, Tommo. Cut it out.

Tommo   Why, I ain't never gonna be a proper politician like this guy, am I?

Sam   I'm not a proper politician.

Michelle   Don't you wanna be though sir?

Sam   No, I . . . I don't know what I . . . (*Beat*). You know, at your age . . . yours isn't the only age where you're going to find you have to make decisions about your life, your future. Your future isn't just something you decide upon when you're young and then one day, bam, it starts. It, it's something that is constantly . . . readdressed.

Shayne   You mean you don't know what you want to be when you go up? (*Laughs*).

Sam (*shrugs*)   No. Actually. I don't.

The bell rings. The students begin to leave.

Sam   OK. Uh . . . listen, sorry I was / late but I'm, I'm glad you got some work done.

Shayne   Fucking hell, that was a long lesson. Thanks sir.

Sam   I'll look over this and . . . and feedback as soon as . . .

*The student all yell 'bye' as they exit, except **Michelle** and **Ray**, who stays seated.*

Michelle (*with the 'Paper'*).   Will it make any difference though, sir? Does anything ever?

Sam   Yes, of . . . everything . . . (*Pause*). I know it feels like things don't change or that, that politics doesn't . . . (*Pause*). No one ever wants to make things worse, politicians don't want . . . we all just disagree on *how*. And I *have* to believe that everyday, in little ways . . . I have to believe that things can get better. That things *are* getting better. That tomorrow will be better than today.

Michelle   Maybe you should become Prime Minister, sir. (*Beat*). Maybe I should . . .

Sam (*smiles*)   You would be an excellent Prime Minister, Michelle.

Michelle *smiles. And exits.* **Sam** *paces, fraught, seemingly forgetting* **Ray**.

Ray   Can I ask you sumfin? Do you hide that you're gay 'cause you're in politics and that?

Sam   I never said I was gay.

Ray   You never said you weren't.

Sam   Well. Um . . . in certain quarters of life, erm . . . tolerance advances slower. Not long ago, teachers couldn't be gay. I'm sure there's perhaps stigma still in, in industry, manufacture. The military, in . . .

Ray   And, like, some families, and that. My family, they're like, Jamaican and well religious, into traditions and all that. My mum would go skitz, bruv. If you get me.

Ray *holds reaches out and rests his hand on* **Sam** *'s.* **Sam** *looks at it.*

Ray   So. Like. Despite what I do. And say. I'm basically asking if you is all right. I'm asking if you're OK. Because what I'm saying is I Get You. Yeah?

Sam *begins to tremble, breaking down as he stares at* **Ray** *'s hand. Overcome.* **Ray** *puts his hand on* **Sam** *'s face.* **Sam** *closes his eyes. Lost. He stands –*

Sam (*exiting*)   Um. Thank-thank you for your work today. Ray. I'm sorry I was late.

Ray   You weren't late, man. Far as I'm concerned, you came right on time.

Sam's Office.

Sam *and* **James**.

James   Well?

Sam (*pause. Shakes his head. Struggling . . .*).

James   OK. I won't bother you again. I'm sorry things aren't easier for you.

Sam   And why do you find everything so pissing easy, ey? Why are you lot supposed to be the liberal 'pioneers', we – I mean us lot, we had the first Lady Prime Minister, shit, probably the first gay Prime Minister, / who knows, so –

James   I'm sure you're right about absolutely everything but I'm leaving, Sam, I'm –

Sam   Our lot brought in gay marriage!, a step even you weren't willing to take last time round. Our guy voted *for* gay adoption, civil partnerships, the repeal of Section 28 when *your* last leader didn't even bother to turn up, for any of them –

James   We didn't make the law; don't take credit for repealing a law that *you* made.

James   You can criticise our record on a lot of things, Jesus, but the one thing, / the One Thing you Cannot criticise us on is this.

Sam   Yeah your lot are so progressive, aren't you; / we had Torch, we have LGBTory, / more gay party members, gay cabinet ministers –

James   What are you doing? What are you hiding behind this – Exactly, Sam, exactly! So who the fuck is stopping you from being happy? Hmm?

The phone rings. **Sam** *and* **James** *stare at each other.*

James   You should answer that. I'll see you, Sam.

James *exits. Beat.* **Sam** *answers the phone. A light on the opposite desk flickers on to reveal* **Ted**, *on the phone. They both sound exhausted.*

Sam   Hello?

Ted   Hello?

Sam (*beat, smiles tragically, shakes his head*)   Hello.

Ted (*looking at his note*)   My apologies, I've been requested to get in touch. Uh . . .

Sam   Where are you, I've . . . I've been trying to find you but I can't, I can't . . . *find* you, I . . .

Ted   Well. I'm just . . . I'm here. (*Pause*). Is there something I can help you with, or . . .?

Sam   I mean, you're, you're very hard to, to . . . *pin* down, to . . . is that, were you looking for something, didn't you know, or were you . . . were you hiding?

Ted   Uh. I don't think I . . . (*Beat*). Hiding, that sounds awful, doesn't it. No.

Sam   Can I ask you . . . what made you choose? When you first began. Why these?

Ted   Um. In truth, I don't think you pick it. I think it picks you –

Sam   Because sometimes . . . sometimes. Just when you think they've moved on . . . when they're on the verge of being . . .

Ted   Well. A friend of mine. Quite the orator. He once said . . . that we have defended ourselves against our enemies. But who will save us from ourselves? So. Why don't you tell me? What made you 'pick a side'?

Sam   Um. I suppose . . . (*Sighs*) . . . I just remember, even as a, as a young . . . man, not even man, just a boy . . . when nothing makes sense, and you're not sure who you are . . . the idea of – the strength of the person that stands alone, carves their own path . . . of it not being who you are or where you're from but what you do, it was . . . I suppose it was that. That bit. That bit made me think it would all be all right.

Ted (*nods*)   Well. Of all the things you should take from this lot, then, I think you should hold to that. If nothing else makes sense, if everything else just seems like a mess. You should hold on to that bit. The bit that makes sense.

Sam (*pause*)   Thank you. (*Beat*). I'm sorry, I have to – I have another call to make. I –

Ted   Yes. Of course. Well. (*Smiles*). Lots to do, lots to do. Goodbye.

They both put the phone down and disappear. **Sam** *picks up his phone and dials.*

Sam   Hi, it's Sam, Michael Daikin's office, a guy called James is about to pass through the lobby, tall, blond hair, could you . . . could you ask him to wait there for just a second? And I'll be right down. Tell him I promise.

Sam's Office.

Sam *stands facing* **Nicholas**, *alone moments before* **Nina** *enters.*

Sam   Can I have a word? Please?

Nicholas   Of course you can, Sam-u-el. Any time.

Nina (*entering*)   Morning, Nick. I've got two / messages for you.

Sam   A proper word. A formal one. It's about the little chat we had.

Nicholas   Yes, of course. Can I just have one minute with Nina, first, and then I'll be right with you.

Pause. **Sam** *exits, passing by* **Robbie** *as he enters.*

Nina   What's going on?

Nicholas (*hushed*)   Right. Here's the – ah, Rob. Perfect. Listen. Um. Listen. You know. . . Sam, I think, is trying to . . . how can I say this, um . . . forward his own agenda. Basically he's going, I think he's going to make a formal complaint. About us.

Nina   About us? What for? Who to?

Nicholas   I don't know, this has come from someone who told me in confidence what Sam told them, which is that he's essentially going to climb on top of us to get where he wants by grinding his axe on the whole 'I'm gay, you're prejudice' bit.

Nina   What? No, that's bullshit?

Nicholas   I'm telling you. Me, you, Michael One, Two. Why would I lie? So if you wouldn't mind standing in on this little chat, just so . . . you know, a united front –

Nina   Erm. OK. Jesus, shouldn't we get Michael Two in, just to –?

Nicholas   No, let's . . . see what he's got to –

Sam (*re-enters*).

Nicholas (*taking post-it's off* **Nina**)   Thank you, Nina. Thank you, thank you. So. Sam?

Sam   Yes, I'd just like a minute please.

Nicholas   Sure. Shoot.

Sam   Alone.

Nicholas   No.

Sam   No?

Nicholas   No. Nein. Nay. C'est impossible. You see, if you're planning on making any formal statements regarding your position here, I feel like I need to have someone else in the room. Standard protocol, you know. Just in case you were about to say something of great weight. In case the whole process of your transfer gets held up while whatever you're about to say is investigated. It might temporarily put a stop on your transit, is what I'm saying. So. In light of that, what is it you would like to discuss with me today, Sam?

Sam (*pause*)   Um . . .

Nicholas   Sam? Anything?

Sam (*pause*)   The, um . . . (*Beat*). I think we should, uh . . . en-enforce an office policy of turning our machines off. Not just on standby. At lunch. And meetings, to set an example. You know? I think that would be a good idea . . .

Nicholas (*smiles. Points at him*)   For you, Samuel? Anything. (*Pause*). Thanks, guys. If that's everything –

Sam   Oh, and there was a message for you from the selection committee. Your candidacy for local councillor is under review.

Nicholas (*laughs*)   What?

Sam   On the grounds of prejudice and discrimination towards a fellow colleague.

Nina   Sam, what are you doing? Is this about all of us?

Sam   No, just him. Rumour has it that he, as my line manager, advised me to seek work in another department on the grounds that I was 'a big queen'.

Nina   What?

Nicholas   He's lying. Thanks, Sam, all right. Who's 'reviewing my candidacy'?

Sam   The deputy fundraising and members chairman for the Putney Association.

Nicholas   Well they don't know what it was we spoke about do they, you fuck. It's just your word against mine, because they weren't there.

Sam   Yes they were.

Nicholas   How where they?

Sam   Because I was there.

Nicholas   And?

Sam (*unfolding a letter*)   And I'm the new deputy fundraising and members chairman for the Putney Association.

Nicholas (*pause. Takes the letter and reads*).

Sam   You were right, Nick, with your reference I was able to get any job I wanted. Thanks for that.

Nicholas   . . .

Sam   Course, they thought I was grossly over qualified but with the incumbent taking immediate leave and what with the selection for new councillors currently in motion they thought I'd better start straight away. My first job is to assess the suitability of candidates. I'm fine on three of them, there's just a black mark against one. A claim of misconduct, doesn't look good. (*At* **Nina** *and* **Robbie**). Of course it will have to be qualified by other colleagues.

Nicholas (*beat. Claps his hands*)   Well bully for you, Miss Fucking Marple.

Nina   Nicholas?

Nicholas   I didn't do anything, OK Nina?! He's making it up! Come on. Rob mate, you're not going to go along with this are you, he's lying.

Robbie   I dunno. You are the guy that asked what my sexuality was on my first morning.

Nicholas . . . (*gasps in disbelief*)   . . . w-what? That was just . . . (*Looks at* **Nina**).

Nina   And I just think you're a bit of a cunt.

Nicholas (*pause. Looks around. Laughs. Stops*)   Sam, come . . . Sammy . . .

Sam *doesn't flinch. Silence.* **Nicholas** *nods his head. Grabs his stuff. Pause.*

Nicholas   Just remember. That I said those things . . . because I wanted to help you. Sam. Because I wanted you to do well. Please at least remember that . . .

Nicholas *leaves. Silence.* **Nina** *and* **Robbie** *break it, laughing.*

Nina   Shit the bed, Sam! I can't believe that. And what's this new job, deputy members –?

Sam   Oh, it doesn't matter, I'm quitting soon.

Robbie   You're what?

Sam   Yeah, just wanted to make sure the right people made it onto the shortlist, then . . .

Nina   And then what? (*Excited*). You staying here?

Sam   Nah, I think it probably is time to move somewhere different, you know.

Robbie   I hear the Prime Minister's position might be vacant soon. You could do that.

Sam (*laughs*)   Well. I'd need to be an MP first.

Ted *appears, standing at his desk with the card drawer open.*
Tim *and* **Frank** *nearby, watching.* **Ted** *takes out one of the cards* . . .

Nina   Well become an MP then, idiot. You'd be ace.

Sam   Mmmdunno. You kind of need more experience first. Like
. . . I don't . . . (*Smiles knowingly*). A local councillor?

Nina   For Wandsworth?!

Sam   Ah-ah-ah. Cards close to your chest in this game, Neen.
(*Looks over to* **Ted**). Cards close to your chest . . .

Ted *looks at* **Sam**. *He smiles, and rips the card, tossing it into the air and exiting with* **Tim** *and* **Frank** *as music grows* . . .

Ray, **Tommo**, **Michelle**, **Adam**, **Muznah**, **Shayne** *and* **Heather**
enter, dancing over to **Sam** *and tossing their own cards into the air.*